The basic book of Macramé and Tatting

The basic book of Macramé and Tatting

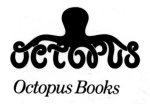

Octopus Books

Macramé articles and materials
by courtesy of Hobby Horse
Limited, London

Photography
by Jason Biggs Studios

First published 1973 by
Octopus Books Limited
59 Grosvenor Street, London W1

ISBN 0 7064 0152 2

Produced by Mandarin Publishers
Filmset by Photoprint Plates Ltd, Essex
Printed in Hong Kong

Contents

Macramé

Macramé–the art of creative knotting–is one of the most ancient crafts known to man. It is known to have been used by the ancient Egyptians, Chinese, Maoris and Peruvians. The tradition of magical, supernatural potency in particular knots has been handed down by sailors through the ages. The origin of the word is a mystery: the Arabic 'migramah' means 'protection, headcovering', while the Turkish 'makrama' is a decoratively fringed napkin. Whatever its origin, old-style macramé lacework was extremely delicate in materials and effect and well established in 13th century Arabia, whence it was carried to Italy via the Moors. Here it flourished during the Middle Ages, but gradually waned, to be revived in a more robust, equally attractive form in the late 19th and early 20th century in and around Turin and Genoa. It is now one of Italy's more popular traditional crafts.

Where teminology varies, an equivalent term is given in [ ].

Learn macramé

What to use

Any yarn can be used to work macramé, depending on the article being made and the finished result required, but the most successful are the smooth, firm yarns which knot easily and do not slip. String is one of the best – and cheapest – materials of all. If you want a crisp finish with the knotting pattern clearly defined, then it is essential you use a firm material such as string, linen thread, nylon cord or any form of cotton. On the other hand if you prefer an all-over textural effect, then any knitting or crochet yarn, fine or thick, can be used. Rug wool is excellent for it is more substantial than ordinary knitting wools, and being thick makes up quickly.

You will need a convenient-sized board to work on for small items, and any oddment of wood – preferably a soft one which will take pins easily – can be used, or a sheet of cork, or even several thicknesses of cardboard. If using a hard wood, it is a good idea to 'pad' it first with a sheet of foam plastic, or even with a folded-up old towel. An expanse of wall makes an ideal working base for large items.

Beginning work

As well as a working surface and a suitable yarn (string is best for practice purposes) you will need some pins, scissors and a tape measure.

Before you can begin knotting, your yarn must be cut into suitable lengths, and these are mounted on to another length of yarn, known as the **holding cord**. This is called **setting [mounting] on threads.** The holding cord is sometimes used as part of the finished design – for instance, as a handle for a bag – or it can be withdrawn after knotting is complete. It is not always easy to join in new yarn in mid-knotting so it is important that working lengths are cut long enough for the complete design. As a very general guide, if setting [mounting] on each thread double (which is the usual method), then the thread should be cut to eight times the length required. For instance, if you are making a braid to measure 6 ins long, then cut each thread 48 ins. If you are setting [mounting] on threads singly, then they should be cut to four times the finished length required.

How to set on [mount] threads

For practice purposes, cut a holding cord of about 12 ins, and 10 lengths of string, each 1 yd long. Tie a knot near one end of the holding cord by taking the end over and round itself and through the loop formed. This is known as an **overhand knot.** Pin the cord through this knot to your working surface near the top left-hand corner. Stretch the cord horizontally across your working surface, tie a similar overhand knot near the other end of the cord and pin it to your working surface. *(fig A)*

Now take the first of your working cords, double it and insert the looped end under the holding cord from top to bottom. Bring the loose ends down over the holding cord and through the loop. Draw tight. Repeat with each length of string, positioning each doubled set-on [mounted] string close to the previous one. When you have finished, you will then have 20 lengths of string hanging vertically from your holding cord, each measuring a little under 18 ins. *(fig B)*

The basic knots

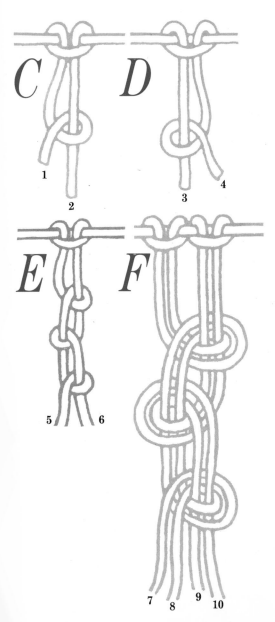

Half hitch

Work on the first 2 cords. To tie a half hitch from the left, hold right-hand cord taut, bring cord 1 in front of it then up and behind it from right to left. Bring through the loop formed. Draw tight. *(fig C)*

Work on cords 3 and 4. To tie a half hitch from the right, merely reverse the knotting procedure: hold left-hand cord taut, and bring right-hand cord in front of it, then up and under it from left to right, and down through loop formed. Draw tight. *(fig D)*

Work on cords 5 and 6: tie a half hitch from the left, then tie a half hitch from the right. Continue in this way, alternating the direction of the knot each time, and drawing each knot close to the previous one. This forms a chain of knots known as the **single alternate half hitch chain.** *(fig E)*

Work on cords 7, 8, 9 and 10. Tie half hitches alternately from the left and right, as for the single alternate half hitch chain, but this time use cords double, so first knot is tied with cords 7 and 8 over 9 and 10; the second knot is tied with cords 9 and 10 over 7 and 8. Continue in this way to form a chain of knots. This is known as the **double alternate half hitch chain**. *(fig F)*

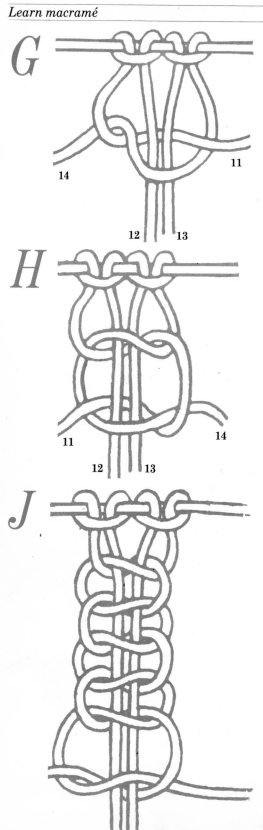

The flat [square] knot

The flat [square] knot which is the second
basic knot is tied in two parts as follows:
work on cords 11, 12, 13 and 14. Hold
cords 12 and 13 taut, take cord 11 under
them and over 14. Take cord 14 over 12
and 13 and under 11. Draw tight. This is
the first half of the flat [square] knot, and
is known as the **half knot.** If the half
knot is tied continuously this produces
an attractive twisted spiral of knots
sometimes called a **sinnet** of flat [square]
knots. *(fig G)*

To complete the flat [square] knot, still
keeping 12 and 13 taut, bring cord 11 back
under 12 and 13 and over 14. Take cord 14
over 12 and 13 and under 11. Draw tight.
(fig H)

Continue in this way to tie flat [square]
knots one below the other to form a
chain. This is often known as a
Solomon's bar. *(fig J)*

K

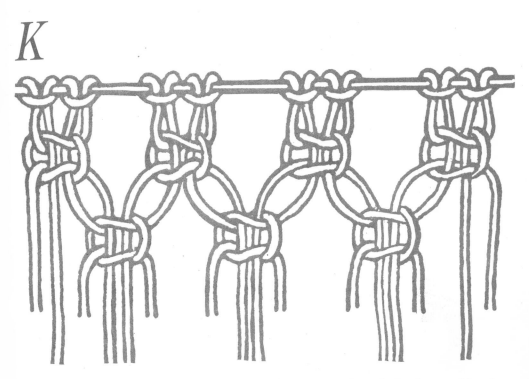

To work the alternate flat [square] knot pattern

This pattern occurs frequently in all forms of macramé work, and is the one most often used to form a fabric. It is worked on any number of knotting cords, provided the total number is a multiple of 4. Begin by tying flat [square] knots with each group of 4 cords to the end of the row. In the 2nd row, leave the first 2 cords unworked, then tie flat [square] knots with each group of 4 cords, to the final 2 cords in the row, leave these 2 cords unworked. The 3rd row is the same as the first, and the 4th row is the same as the 2nd. Continue in this way to build up a fabric. By tying knots and rows close together you create a dense fabric; space out knots and rows and you will achieve an open-work lacy fabric. (*fig K*)

Cording

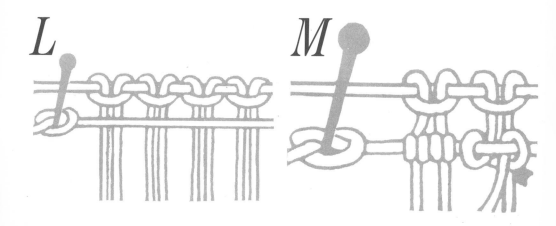

This is a useful macramé technique, for it can be used to create solid fabrics, to 'draw' outlines and figures, and to shape edges of work. It is based on the half hitch knot.

To practise cording on your set-on [mounted] strings, cut a new length of string, approximately 1 yd long. Tie an overhand knot near one end of it, and pin it to your working surface immediately to the left of working cords. Lay it horizontally across working cords. This is known as a leader cord, and as the knots are all tied on to this leader cord, it is essential that it is kept taught all the time – if necessary pin it to your working surface at the opposite side to kept it taut while you work. *(fig L)*

Now beginning with cord 1, take it up and over leader, and then down behind it, bringing end out to the left of the loop formed. Repeat sequence exactly with the same cord – this means you have tied 2 half hitches, or – as is more usually known – a double half hitch. Repeat with every cord along the row, pushing each half hitch as it is tied close to the previous one. At the end of the row you should have a row of tiny loops along the leader cord all nestling close to each other. *(fig M)*

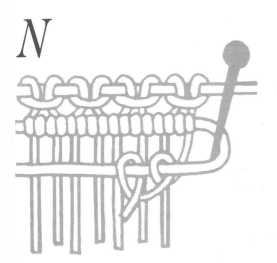

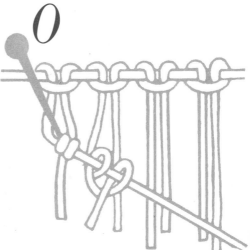

To work the next row, place a pin in working surface close to the end of the first row, take leader round the pin and place it horizontally across working cords, this time from right to left. Now tie double half hitches with each cord in turn, but this time as you are working from right to left, as each half hitch is tied you will bring the cord end down to the right of the loop formed. This is known as horizontal cording. *(fig N)*

Diagonal cording is worked in a similar way, except leader cord is placed at an angle across working cords. The leader for horizontal or diagonal cording may be a separate cord, as here, or it can be one of the set-on [mounted] cords. *(fig O)*

Tie belt

Materials: Jute, or similar mediumweight soft string; 16 oval wooden beads; long wooden beads (number will depend on size of belt required).

Measurements: Belt is intended as a loose-fitting tie belt, and can be made to any length to suit size of waist. The centre pattern section should equal size of waist plus 4 ins. Beaded tie at each end should equal approximately 9 ins.

Tension (gauge) check: Chain [sinnet] of 7 flat [square] knots measures 1 in.

Preparation: Cut 16 cords to equal 4 times the total length of belt required, including ties at each end. (*Note:* As cords are cut singly for this design, it is necessary only to cut to 4 times the total finished length required, instead of usual 8 times.)
Lay cords side by side on your working surface. Divide cords into pairs and thread an oval bead on to each pair. Tie an overhand knot close to ends of cords to prevent bead slipping off.
Leave a space of about 1½ ins below bead then using cord on far left as leader work diagonal cording slanting down to the right with all cords.

To make
Continuing with same cord as leader work 3 more rows of diagonal cording to form a very wide zig-zag, with big areas of unworked cords between each row (*see illustration*). After the 4th row of the zig-zag has been worked, total length of work (including beads) should measure about 9 ins.

1st pattern panel
With cord on far left as leader work horizontal cording from left to right across all cords. Reverse direction of leader round a pin, and work a 2nd row of horizontal cording this time from right to left, immediately below the first. Divide cords into 4 groups of 4 cords each. With each group work a flat [square] knot chain to about 1½ ins.
Cross first chain over 2nd, and cross 4th chain over 3rd. Pin them if necessary to hold in place so cords line up, then with cord on far left as leader work a double row of horizontal cording as before across all cords.

2nd pattern panel

With cord on far left as leader work a row of
diagonal cording slanting only slightly down
to the right with first 7 cords. In a similar way
work a row of diagonal cording slanting down
to the left, using cord on far right as leader,
and knotting over it the 7 cords on right-hand
side of work.

With cord on far left as leader work a 2nd row
of diagonal cording immediately below the
first knotting over it all the cords on this side
of work (including leader from previous row).
In a similar way work a 2nd row of diagonal
cording on right-hand side of work.

Take centre 2 cords through a long wooden
bead.

Let remaining cords curve gently round the
bead on either side – do not pull them too
tightly, or – on the other hand – allow them to
form too large curves.

With cord immediately to the left of the bead
as leader slanting down to the left, work
diagonal cording over it with all cords at left-
hand side of work. Work a 2nd row of diagonal
cording immediately below, using left-hand
cord of pair threaded through bead as leader,
and knotting over it all cords on the left,
including leader from previous row.

In a similar way work a double row of
diagonal cording slanting down to the right
with cords at right-hand side of work. * * Now
repeat from * to * * until belt is required
length, excluding tie at other end. Finish after
a first pattern panel.

To finish

Using cord on far left as leader work 4 rows of
zig-zag diagonal cording to match zig-zag at
beginning of work. Finish with an oval bead
on each pair of cords, and tie an overhand
knot beneath each bead to hold in place.

Shopping bag

Materials: Mediumweight parcel string; 2 wooden rings, each with a diameter of $3\frac{1}{2}$ ins.

Measurements: Finished bag measures very approximately 12 ins deep by 13 ins wide, at widest point, but can be made to any size wished.

Tension (gauge) check: A chain [sinnet] of 5 flat [square] knots measures 1 in.

Preparation: Cut 20 cords each 16 ft (or 16 times finished length of bag required). Double these cords and pin them by their top loops, side by side on your working surface. Work chains of 2 flat [square] knots with each group of 4 cords. Unpin the chains from your working surface. Wind cords from each chain once round one of the wooden rings, having knotted sections at base of ring. Bring unworked cord ends down through centre of cords and draw tight. Repeat with each chain until all are set on [mounted] to the wooden ring. The 2-knot chains should now lie on wrong side of ring, the cord ends, ready for knotting, should be at front of work.

To make

On first 4 cords work a chain of 10 flat [square] knots; then work a 6-knot chain with each group of 4 cords to last 4 cords; work a chain of 10 flat [square] knots with these last 4 cords.

Work now continues in the alternate flat [square] knot pattern until bag is size required. However, as the bag is made 'in the round' you will not be able to work on your normal flat working surface; instead a suitable three-dimensional working base must be used.

As shaping for this bag is achieved entirely by adjusting knotting to fit the base, it is important to choose one which will give you the right finished shape and size of bag. A round glass lampshade (the globe variety) will do very well provided it is big enough; an upturned pudding basin could also be used; or a large rubber ball; or even a goldfish bowl. Padding your surface with foam plastic or a similar substance will give you a surface to pin your work to, and can also help to give you a more accurate size and shape of base. Work continues in the alternate flat [square]

r colour illustration, see page 19

knot pattern, with shaping achieved to match
working base by increasing and decreasing
distance between knots and rows of knots.
The pattern is intended to be an open-work
lacy one, so it does not matter – within reason
– how big you make the distance between
knots and rows. Side edges should be curved
gently outwards to give shape as shown in the
picture of the finished bag on page 19. To give
increased strength to these edges work double
knots instead of single ones on each row, and
have 4 central knotbearing core cords (this
will include 2 cords from the next knot along).
Shaping should be such that side edges stop
somewhere around the midway point of total
length of bag required; main knotting continues to total depth in centre, gradually
decreasing out to meet side edges.

When the first side of the bag is complete continue knotting round other side of your working base to make a 2nd side of similar size and
shaping to the first. This time, of course, knotting will progress from base of bag towards
the top. If knotbearing core cords along side
edges are constantly pulled tight this will help
to draw in side edges even more, and give
better shaping to rest of bag.

When the 2 sides of the bag match up as far as
the flat [square] knot chains at beginning,
stop alternate flat [square] knot pattern, and
end with flat [square] knot chains to match
those worked at the beginning.

To finish

With right side of work face upwards, lay
wooden ring over cord ends coming from flat
[square] knot chains. Take the 4 cords coming
from first chain and bring them down over the
wooden ring, then divide in 2 pairs and take
left-hand pair to back of work to left of flat
[square] knot chain, take right-hand pair to
back of work to right of flat [square] knot
chain. Turn work over, and tie these 4 ends
together in a chain of 2 flat [square] knots. Tie
knots tightly against wooden ring to prevent
it slipping too much. Repeat with each group
of cords to end.

Trim cord ends neatly.

(*Note:* If it is preferred not to work this design
three-dimensionally, the bag may be made in 2
separate sections, then the sections stitched
together round side and lower edges. This
will not give such a pleasing rounded and
capacious bag, however. Also, there will be
the problem of dealing neatly with ends along
lower edge of bag – this can be solved by com-
bining cords from each side into multiple
tassels.)

String and bead choker

Materials: Mediumweight parcel string; 31 long wooden beads.

Measurements: Length from centre back fastening round to centre front drop approximately 12 ins; width at sides of choker (excluding beads) approximately 2 ins.

Tension (gauge) check: Chain [sinnet] of 7 flat [square] knots measures 1 in.

Preparation: *Note:* Each side of the choker is made separately then the 2 strips are joined at centre front.

For left-hand side strip: Cut 2 lengths of string, each 8 ft. Double these together and pin to working surface by their top loops. With cord on far left as knotting cord, begin about an inch down from the double top loop and work half hitches over the cord next to it. Work upwards to top of loop then continue down right-hand side. Finish beside point where you began, to give a complete loop of half hitches (sometimes known as a button-hole loop).

You now have 4 knotting cords hanging down from the buttonhole loop: with these work a half knot spiral (tie the first half of the flat [square] knot continuously) for about 2 ins.

for colour illustration, see page 22

Now cut 4 new lengths of string, each 7 ft. Lay these together, and place them on your working surface so their midway point is under the 4 knotting cords from spiral just worked. Knot the new cords once round the knotting cords. Work a flat [square] knot immediately below with the 4 central knotting cords to hold the new cords in place. In a similar way introduce another 2 new cords, each cut to 7 ft on to the 4 central cords. You should now have a total of 16 cords, arranged in groups of 4, 2, 4, 2 and 4.

For right-hand side strip: Cut 2 lengths of string, each 8 ft. Place both lengths together, and thread a bead on to the double thickness, positioning it at the midway point. Tie a flat [square] knot immediately below with the 4 knotting cords to hold bead in place. Pin to your working surface through the flat [square] knot, then work a half knot spiral for about 2 ins. Complete preparation for this side strip exactly as for left-hand side strip.

To make

Work on left-hand side strip first: With cords 1–4 work a half knot spiral for about 1½ ins. Thread cords 5 and 6 on to a bead; tie a double half hitch with cord 6 over cord 5 immediately below to hold the bead in place. Work a flat [square] knot chain with cords 7–10 for about 1 in.

(*Note:* As half knot spiral worked with first 4 cords has to be curved round slightly in order to bring its working cords into line with the others, by working the central flat [square] knot chain to only about 1 in this should bring cords into line.)

Thread cords 11 and 12 on to a bead; tie a double half hitch with cord 12 over cord 11 immediately below to hold the bead in place.

Work a half knot spiral for about 1½ ins with cords 12–16.

Begin cording pattern: With cord on the far left as leader, work horizontal cording from left to right across all cords.

Now, using cord on the far left as leader throughout, work a zig-zag of diagonal cording leaving areas of unworked cords between each row of the zig-zag. Use the same leader cord throughout – odd numbered rows will therefore be worked from left to right; even numbered rows from right to left. After you have worked the 9th row of diagonal cording (from left to right), still using the same leader, work next 2 rows of diagonal cording on 11 cords only (leaving 4 cords at left-hand side of work unworked).

Next row (right to left): Work across all cords.

Work on right-hand side strip: Work exactly as for left-hand side strip, but begin diagonal cording with cord on far right as leader. After 9th row work 2 rows of cording on 11 cords at left-hand side of work, leaving 4 right-hand cords unworked.

Link 2 side strips: Place both worked strips on your working surface side by side so working cords line up.

Now cross cord on far right of left-hand strip over cord on far left of right-hand strip. Using cord from left-hand strip as leader work diagonal cording over it with first 7 cords of right-hand strip.

In a similar way work diagonal cording over cord from right-hand side with first 6 cords of left-hand strip.

Work on the centre 12 cords (coming from cording rows just worked):

1st row: Tie 1 flat [square] knot with centre 4 cords.

2nd row: Bringing in 2 cords at either side, tie 2 flat [square] knots.

3rd row: Bring in 2 more cords at either side, and tie 3 flat [square] knots.

4th row: Leave first 2 cords unworked, tie 2 flat [square] knots, leave final 2 cords unworked.

Now cut 2 new cords each about 6 ins. Lay one of these new cords across 16 cords at left-hand side of work, and beginning 2 ins from the end of this cord, work cording over it with each of the 16 cords in turn to form lower edge. Work from left to right, and begin row at left-hand edge of final row of diagonal cording worked on left-hand strip.

In a similar way use 2nd new cord to work cording across 16 cords on right-hand side of work. Link these 2 leaders at centre of work by knotting left-hand leader over right-hand leader.

To finish

Divide cords along lower edge in pairs and thread a bead on to each pair of cords. Tie an overhand knot below each bead to hold it in place, and trim cord ends.

Cut 8 cords, each about 4 ins. Set [mount] 2 of these cords on to the 3rd 'loop' of the cording zig-zag at left-hand edge of left side strip. Set [mount] another 2 cords on to zig-zag loop immediately below. In a similar way set on [mount] remaining 4 cords to right-hand edge of right side strip.

Work on first set of 4 cords: Tie a flat [square] knot with the 4 cords, then divide cords into 2 pairs, thread a bead on to each pair, and tie an overhand knot to hold in place. Trim cords.

Repeat with each of other 3 groups of 4 cords.

Beaded sampler bag

Materials: Heavyweight parcel string.
16 oval glass beads.

Measurements: Finished bag measures
approximately 11½ ins square, excluding
fringe.

Tension (gauge) check: Chain [sinnet] of 4
flat [square] knots measures 1 in.

Preparation: Each side of the bag is made
alike. For each side therefore cut 36 cords,
each 8 ft long plus measurement of fringe
required. Set [mount] these on to a holding
cord of about 18 in.

To make: With cord on far left as leader
work a row of horizontal cording across all
all cords.

1st pattern panel

With first 4 cords, work a chain of 8 flat
[square] knots. Work on next group of 12
cords: with cord 1 as leader slanting down to
the right, work diagonal cording over it with
cords, 2, 3, 4, 5 and 6. With cord 2 as leader
work a 2nd row of diagonal cording immediately below the first with cords, 3, 4, 5, 6 and 1.
In a similar way work a double row of
diagonal cording slanting down to the left
with cord 12 as leader for first row, cord 11
leader for 2nd row.
Link 4 central cords by tying together in a
single flat [square] knot. Now let cord 2 continue as leader slanting down to the left and
work diagonal cording over it with cords 1, 6,
5, 4 and 3. With cord 1 as leader slanting down
to the left work a 2nd row of diagonal cording

for colour illustration, see page 23

immediately below with cords 6, 5, 4, 3 and 2.
Complete right-hand side of motif by working
a double row of diagonal cording slanting
down to the right with cord 11 as leader for
the first row, cord 12 leader for 2nd row.
With next 4 cords, work a chain of 8 flat
[square] knots. Work on next group of 14
cords: tie a flat [square] knot with first 4
cords, then tie a flat [square] knot with cords
3, 4, 5 and 6, then tie another flat [square]
knot with cords 1, 2, 3 and 4. Tie a flat [square]
knot with cords 11, 12, 13 and 14, then tie a
flat [square] knot with cords 9, 10, 11 and
12, and then tie another flat [square] knot
with cords 13. 14, 15 and 16. Now using cord 7
as a leader slanting down to the left work
diagonal cording over it with cords, 6, 5, 4, 3,
2 and 1. Similarly with cord 8 as leader slanting to the right, work diagonal cording over it
with cords 9, 10, 11, 12, 13 and 14. Weave cords
in centre of motif (i.e., all cords except
leaders) over and under each other to form a
criss-cross lattice pattern as shown in illustration on page 23. Complete diamond motif by
working rows of diagonal cording beneath lattice pattern. Use cord 7 as leader for left-hand
row; cord 8 leader for right-hand row.
Tie a flat [square] knot with cords 1, 2, 3 and 4,
then tie a flat [square] knot with cords 3, 4, 5
and 6. Similarly tie a flat [square] knot with
cords 11, 12, 13 and 14, then tie a flat [square]
knot with cords 9, 10, 11 and 12. With next 4
cords work a spiral of 20 half knots (first half
of the flat [square] knot tied continuously).
Complete pattern panel to match section
already worked: i.e., work lattice-work pattern motif with next 14 cords, then flat
[square] knot chain with 4 cords, followed by
criss-cross of double rows of cording with 12
cords, and finally a flat [square] knot
chain with 4 cords.

Divider row: With cord on far left as leader, work a row of horizontal cording across all cords.

2nd pattern panel

Divide cords into groups of 9 cords each.
Work on first group of 9 cords: * with cord on far left as leader slanting down to the right work diagonal cording with all cords in the group.
Work on next group of 9 cords: with cord on far right as leader slanting down to the left work diagonal cording over it with all cords in group. * *
Repeat from * to * * to end of row.
Now tie a flat [square] knot at the lower point of each cording row so cording rows are linked together in pairs. Tie a flat [square] knot at the top of cording rows, again linking 2 cords from one row with the 2 cords from row next to it. Work on first linked motif only: tie a flat [square] knot with first 4 cords, then a flat [square] knot with cords 3, 4, 5 and 6, then tie a flat [square] knot with cords, 5, 6, 7 and 8.
Take cords 9 and 10 through a bead, then complete row by tying flat [square] knots in turn with cords 11, 12, 13 and 14; 13, 14, 15 and 16; 15, 16, 17 and 18.
Tie a flat [square] knot below bead with cords 8, 9, 10 and 11. Work diagonal cording down left-hand side of motif with cord 1 as leader, and cords 2–9 as knotting cords. Work diagonal cording down right-hand side of motif with cord 18 as leader, and cords 17–10 as knotting cords. Complete other motifs across row in a similar way.
Now return to first 4 cords and work a chain of 14 flat [square] knots.
On next 5 cords work a 4-row zig-zag of diagonal cording, using cord on the far right

as leader for each row.
Work on next group of 18 cords: tie cords 8, 9, 10 and 11 in a spiral of 20 half knots.
Tie cords 4, 5, 6 and 7 in a spiral of 10 half knots; tie cords 12, 13, 14 and 15 in a spiral of 10 half knots.
With cord 1 as leader slanting down to the right (leader from row of cording previously worked) work diagonal cording with cords 2–9. With cord 18 as leader slanting down to the left work diagonal cording with cords 17–10.
Now work cords on right-hand side of work to correspond with left-hand patterns worked: i.e., working from right to left, flat [square] knot chain; zig-zag of cording; diamond motif of half knot spirals.
Now work on cords at centre of work; letting cord already being used as leader for diagonal cording slanting down to the left continue as leader, continue diagonal cording at same slant knotting over the leader the cords coming from lower right-hand side of half knot spiral diamond.
In a similar way continue row of diagonal cording slanting down to the right on right of central cords.
Begin at tip of inverted 'V' of cording in centre and tie a single flat [square] knot (2 cords from each side). Work in alternate flat [square] knot pattern, bringing in 2 new cords at each end of every row until finally the row is worked using all cords and lining up with end of cording rows.
Continue in alternate flat [square] knot pattern, this time dropping 2 cords at each end of every row until finally the row is worked with only 1 flat [square] knot in it. You should now have completed a central diamond of alternate flat [square] knot pattern. Complete diamond with a cording row down each of remaining

sides, using same leaders as before.
Complete remainder of pattern panel to correspond with section already worked: i.e., 2
more half knot spiral diamonds (one each side
of central flat [square] knot diamond); then
cording, flat [square] knot and beaded motifs.
Divider row: As first divider row.

3rd pattern panel

Work as for first pattern panel.
Divider row: As first divider row.
Work 2nd side of bag in a similar way.

To make handle

Cut 2 cords, each 16 ft, plus 8 times the length
of finished handle required, plus double the
measurement of fringe required (i.e., if you
wish a handle of 3 ft, and a fringe round lower
edge of bag of 6 in, cut handle cords to
16+24+1 ft, which equals 41 ft).
Double these cords and pin them to your
working surface. Measure down from their
top loops the depth of fringe you require, then
begin knotting from this point. Work a chain
of flat [square] knots to a depth of about 11½
in, then continue working in half knot spirals
to the measurement of handle required. Finish
with a chain of flat [square] knots to 11½ in.

To finish

Trim leader cords to about 1 in of knotting.
Press to back of work and secure with a few
neat stitches. Place both sides of bag together,
wrong sides facing. Position handle so flat
[square] knot chains form sides of bag, and
spirals form handle. Stitch firmly in position.
Now divide cords along lower edge of bag into
groups of 8 (4 cords from back with 4 cords
from front). Tie these groups into tassels, as
described in To finish section of Small
sampler bag (see page 30). Trim ends evenly.
(*Note:* Instead of stitching final assembly of
bag, handle may be worked directly in place
by looping knotting cords in flat [square] knot
chains round loops at row ends on main bag
sections in between each flat [square] knot in
the chain, thus linking side sections to main
sections as you knot.)

Small sampler bag

Materials: Heavyweight parcel string.

Measurements: Length of bag (excluding fringe and handle) 9¾ ins; width 8½ ins.

Tension (gauge) check: 4 flat [square] knots measure 1 in.

Preparation: *Note:* Each side of the bag is made in the same way. For each side therefore, cut 26 cords each 88 ins. Set [mount] these on to a holding cord of about 14 ins.

To make: With cord on far left as leader, work a row of horizontal cording across all cords.

1st pattern panel

With first 6 cords, work a chain of 6 flat [square] knots. Work on next 8 cords: slant first of the 8 cords down to the right and work a row of diagonal cording with remaining 7 cords over the first cord as leader. Arrange slant of leader so cording row lines up with base of flat [square] knot chain already worked. With next 4 cords work a spiral of half knots (first half of the flat [square] knot tied continuously). Stop spiral at same depth as flat [square] knot chain and diagonal cording row already worked. With each of next 2 groups of 4 cords, work a chain of 7 flat [square] knots. With next 4 cords, work a spiral of half knots to same depth as previous spiral of half knots. With each of next 2 groups of 4 cords, work a chain of 7 flat [square] knots. With next 4 cords, work a spiral of half knots.

Work on next 8 cords: slant last of the 8 cords down to the left and use as leader for a row of diagonal cording, knotting other 7 cords over this leader cord.

With last 4 cords, work a chain of 6 flat knots. Now cross each pair of adjoining flat [square] knot chains over each other, as shown in illustration. Pin to hold in place.

Divider rows: With cord on far left as leader work a row of horizontal cording across all cords. Reverse direction of leader around a pin, and work a 2nd row of horizontal cording immediately below.

for colour illustrations, see pages 27 and 31

2nd pattern panel

Work on first group of 8 cords: Work a chain of 3 flat [square] knots with each group of 4 cords. Link the 2 chains by knotting right-hand 2 cords of left-hand chain with left-hand 2 cords of right-hand chain in a single flat [square] knot. Work a further 3 flat [square] knots with first 4 cords, and with 2nd 4 cords. Work on next group of 16 cords: work in alternate flat [square] knot pattern, keeping left-hand edge straight, and dropping 2 cords from right-hand edge on each row until row with only 1 flat [square] knot in it is worked.

Now work on right-hand cords to correspond with left-hand side already worked: i.e., working from right-hand side in – 2 chains of linked flat [square] knots, followed by alternate flat [square] knot pattern over 16 cords, right-hand edge kept straight, with a slanting left-hand edge.

Now work on central panel thus: with cord 17 as leader slanting to the left, work a row of diagonal cording across all cords from alternate flat [square] knot pattern section. With cord 18 as leader, work a 2nd row of diagonal cording immediately below this first one. In a similar way work a double row of diagonal cording slanting down to the right with cords 19 and 20.

Now fill in central diamond of half knot spirals. Divide cords coming from diagonal cording rows into groups of 4, so central spiral will be tied with 2 cords from the left, 2 from the right. You will then have 3 spirals on either side of this central spiral, with an odd unworked cord at either end. Central spiral will have 32 half knots tied in it (allow spiral to twist round itself after every 4th knot); first spirals on either side of central spiral will each have 28 knots; spirals either side of this will have 24 knots; and final 2 spirals at either

end will have 16 knots.

Now let cord 18 continue as leader. Reverse its direction round a pin, and let it slant down to the right. Work diagonal cording over it with all cords on left-hand side of diamond. Work a 2nd row of diagonal cording immediately below.

In a similar way work a double row of diagonal cording down right-hand side of diamond with cords 19 and 20 as leaders.

Now complete lower part of pattern panel to correspond with upper part so you have linked chains of flat [square] knots, and diamonds of alternate flat [square] knot patterns. Link the single knot of the alternate flat [square] knot triangle to the flat [square] knot chains next to it by tying a single flat [square] knot with 2 cords of each.

Divider rows: As previous divider rows.

3rd pattern panel

On first 4 cords, work a chain of 6 flat [square] knots. Work on next 8 cords: work a cross-over of diagonal cording thus – with cord 1 as leader slanting down to the right, work diagonal cording over it with cords 2, 3 and 4. Similarly with cord 8 as leader slanting down to the left, work diagonal cording over it with cords 7, 6 and 5. Now link the central point of the cross-over by tying a flat [square] knot with the 4 central cords. Renumber cords in the position in which they now lie from 1–8. With cord 4 as leader slanting down to the left work diagonal cording over it with cords 3, 2 and 1. With cord 5 as leader slanting down to the right, work diagonal cording over it with cords 6, 7 and 8. With each of next 2 groups of 4 cords, work chains of 2 flat [square] knots. Link the chains by tying 2 right-hand cords of chain 1 with 2 left hand cords of chain 2 in a single flat [square] knot. Then continue with chains as before, 2 flat [square] knots in each chain.

Work on next 6 cords: with cord 6 as leader slanting down to the left, work diagonal cording over it with cords 5, 4, 3, 2 and 1. With cord 5 as leader slanting down to the left, work a 2nd row of diagonal cording slanting down to the left immediately below the first, knotting over it cords 4, 3, 2 and 1. Now reverse direction of cord 5 round a pin and work diagonal cording slanting down to the right knotting over it cords 1, 2, 3 and 4. Similarly, reverse direction of cord 6 round a pin and knot over it cords 1, 2, 3, 4 and 5. Complete rest of pattern panel to correspond with first part, reversing direction of patterns as required.

Divider rows: As first divider rows.
Work 2nd half of bag in a similar way.

To make handle

Cut 2 cords, each $5\frac{1}{2}$ yds plus 8 times the length of finished handle required. Double these cords and pin them to your working surface. Begin knotting about 9 ins below top loops of cords. Work a flat [square] knot chain to a depth of about $9\frac{3}{4}$ ins. Now work in half knot spirals until handle is length required. Finish with a chain of flat [square] knots to $9\frac{3}{4}$ ins.

To finish

Trim leader cords to about 1 in of knotting. Press to back of work, and secure with a few neat stitches. Place both sides of bag together, wrong sides facing. Position handle so flat [square] knot chains form sides of bag, and spirals form handle. Stitch firmly in position. Now divide cords along lower edge of bag into groups of 8 (4 cords from back with 4 cords from front). Tie these groups into tassels: take one of the cords, and form a loop in front of other cords in group. Take it round the group from left to right and them down through loop. Draw tight. Repeat 4 more times. Trim cord ends evenly.

Sampler wall hanging

Materials: Heavyweight parcel string; assorted glass and china beads.

Measurements: Hanging measures approximately 22 ins long, excluding fringe; 10 ins wide.

Tension (gauge) check: A chain [sinnet] of 3 flat [square] knots measures 1 in.

Preparation: Cut 22 cords, each 16 ft, plus length of fringe required. Set [mount] these on to a holding cord of about 24 ins.

To make: With cord on far left as leader, work a row of horizontal cording across all cords.

1st pattern panel

With first 4 cords, work a chain of 4 flat [square] knots. Work on next group of 8 cords: with cord 1 as leader slanting down to the right, work diagonal cording over it with cords 2, 3 and 4. Similarly slant cord 8 down to the left and work diagonal cording over it with cords 7, 6 and 5. Link the 2 leaders at this central point by looping one around the other. Cord 1 now continues as leader and is slanted down to the left. Work diagonal cording over it with cords 4, 3 and 2. Complete criss-cross of cording by working diagonal cording slanting down to the right with cords 5, 6 and 7 over cord 8.

With next 4 cords, work a chain of 4 flat [square] knots. Work on next group of 6 cords: work 3 rows of diagonal cording slanting down the left, each row immediately below the previous one. First row will have cord 4 as leader, and cords 3, 2 and 1 will be knotted over it. In the 2nd row, cord 5 is leader, and cords 3, 2, 1 and 4 are knotting cords. In the 3rd row, cord 6 is leader, and cords 3, 2, 1, 4 and 5 are knotting cords.

Now complete remainder of pattern panel to correspond with section already worked, reversing direction of triple row cording motif.

Divider row: With cord on far left as leader, work a row of horizontal cording across all cords.

for colour illustration, see page 35

2nd pattern panel

Work in alternate flat [square] knot pattern
for 7 rows. After the first row, drop 2 cords on
each row at outside edges. After the 3rd row,
leave centre 4 cords unworked, then drop 4
further cords in the centre with each subse-
quent row, so you eventually have a 'W' shape
of alternate flat [square] knot pattern. Final
row should have only 2 flat [square] knots in it
– one knot in each tip of the 'W'.

With cord on far left as leader slanting down
to the right work diagonal cording over it
with all cords coming from left-hand side of
the 'W'.

Similarly work a row of diagonal cording
down the right-hand side of the 'W', using
cord on far right of work as leader. Work rows
of diagonal cording in a similar way down
each of the inside edges of the 'W', using left-
hand central cord as leader for left-hand row;
right-hand central cord as leader for right-
hand row.

Take 4 cords now lying in centre of work (2
from left-hand cording row just worked, 2
from right-hand row). Work a spiral of 16 half
knots (first half of the flat [square] knot tied
continuously). With 4 cords on left of this
spiral, work a spiral of 8 half knots. With 4
cords on right of centre spiral, work another
spiral of 8 half knots.

Now with same leaders as before work
diagonal cording beneath spirals just worked,
to complete central diamond motif. Now complete pattern panel to match section already
worked, working a row of diagonal cording at
each side of panel first, with same leaders as
before, then filling in remaining area with the
alternate flat [square] knot pattern.

Divider row: As previous divider row.

3rd pattern panel

With centre 4 cords work a half knot spiral of
24 knots. Now go back to top left-hand corner
of work. With cord 2nd from the left as leader
slanting down to the right work a row of
diagonal cording with all cords on left-hand
side of work. Stop cording row at midway
point of central spiral already worked (i.e. the
2 left-hand cords of spiral will be used as knotting cords for the diagonal cording).

Work a 2nd row of cording immediately below
this first one, using cord on far left of work as
leader. Use same knotting cords as in previous
row.

In a similar way work a double row of
diagonal cording down right-hand side of
work.

Link the 4 cords now lying in centre of work
(i.e. leaders from cording rows) by tying them
in a single flat knot. Return to cords on left-
hand side of work.

Work on first 6 cords: Work a 4-row zig-zag of
diagonal cording, using cord 6 as leader
throughout. End of 4th row of the zig-zag
should line up with linked point of central 'V'
of cording.

Work on next 4 cords: With central 2 cords as
the knotbearing core, work a chain of
reversed double half hitches from right and
left alternately.

To work a reversed double half hitch: Keep
central knotbearing core cords taut, as for a
flat [square] knot, then tie a half hitch from
the left across the knotbearing cords with
cord 1.

Complete the knot by taking cord 1 under the
knotbearing cords, then up and across them
from right to left, then down through the loop
formed. Draw tight. This completes one
reversed double half hitch worked from the
left.

To work the knot from the right, use cord 4 as knotting cord, and work sequence as given above, but working half hitch from the right across knotbearing cords then taking knotting cord under them, and up and across them from left to right.

A chain of reversed double half hitches tied alternately from the left and right is sometimes known as a tatted bar. Work 9 reversed double half hitches altogether, which should bring chain level with zig-zag of cording already worked.

Now work on next group of 8 cords: With first 4 cords tie a chain of 2 flat [square] knots; with 2nd group of 4 cords tie 1 flat [square] knot. Now link these 2 sets of cords by tying a multi-end flat [square] knot – i.e., you will have double knotting cords, and a central knotbearing core of 4 cords.

Divide into 2 groups of 4 cords each again, and work a single flat [square] knot with each group. Link groups as before in 1 multi-end flat [square] knot. Complete right-hand side of work to correspond with left-hand pattern.

Divider row: As first divider row.

4th pattern panel

On first 4 cords, work a tatted bar, with a total of 12 reversed double half hitches.

Work a similar tatted bar with 4 final cords in row.

Now work on central cords: Work 1 row of flat [square] knots across all cords. Now divide into 2 equal groups and continue in the alternate flat [square] knot pattern on each group, dropping 2 cords at each end of every row to form a 'V' of pattern. Work diagonal cording down each side of the 'V' shapes, using cord on far left as leader for left-hand row; cord on far right as leader for right-hand row. Complete 2nd 'V' in a similar way.

Work on cords in centre of work (coming from 2 centre rows of diagonal cording just worked). Weave these cords over and under each other to form a criss-cross lattice pattern, as shown in photograph on page 35.

With same leaders as before, reverse their directions round pins and work a row of diagonal cording below lattice pattern to form a central diamond motif.

Work 2 final rows of diagonal cording to complete pattern panel, using same leaders as before to the left and right of central diamond motif, and reversing their directions round pins.

Divider row: As first divider row.

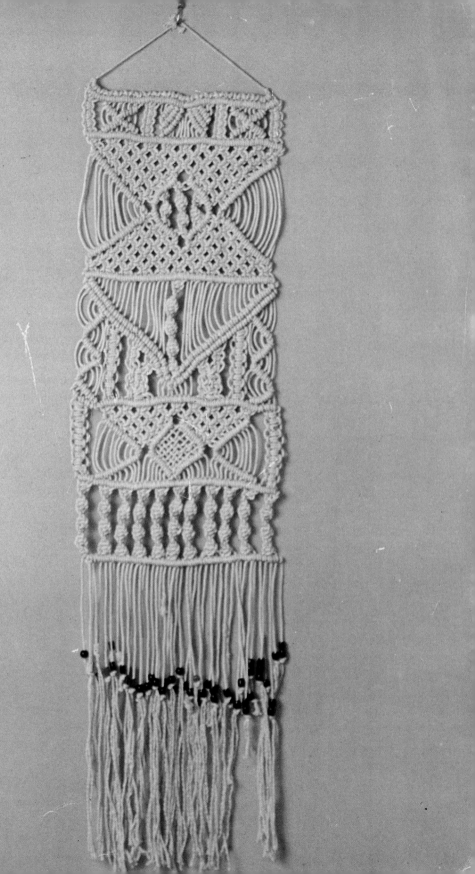

5th pattern panel

Divide cords into groups of 4 cords each. On each group work a half knot spiral with 20 half knots in each spiral.

Divider row: As first divider row.

To finish

Thread a bead on to each cord end, positioning bead where you wish on the cord, then tying an overhand knot below to secure. Trim cord ends to length required and fray out ends below beads if wished.

Untie overhand knots in holding cord, and tie ends of holding cord together so complete hanging may be hung on the wall.

(*Note:* If wished, cords for this design may be set on [mounted] directly to a length of wooden rod, to give a more substantial heading for the design.)

Child's purse

Materials: Mediumweight parcel string (dyed, if wished); large and small china beads.

Measurements: Finished purse measures approximately 4½ ins square.

Tension (gauge) check: 9 rows of alternate flat [square] knot pattern measures 1 in.

Preparation: Cut 28 cords, each 7 ft. Set [mount] these on to a holding cord approximately 10 ins long. You now have 56 working ends.

for colour illustration, see page 39

To make

Work in the alternate flat [square] knot pattern for 2 rows, keeping knots and rows fairly close together to give a dense fabric. Now divide cords into 2 equal groups, each of 28 cords. Work on left-hand group first: Continue to work in alternate flat [square] knot pattern, but drop 2 cords on the right-hand side on each row. Keep left-hand edge straight. You will thus work one knot fewer each row until finally you work a row with only one flat [square] knot in it. You should have formed a triangular shape of flat [square] knot pattern. In a similar way work a triangular shape of alternate flat [square] knot pattern with cords at right-hand side of work, but in this case keep right-hand edge straight, and drop cords 2 at a time on each row from left-hand edge. Work central beaded panel: With cord on far right of left-hand triangle as leader work diagonal cording slanting down to the left with all cords from left-hand side of work. Work cording close to flat [square] knots to form an edge for the triangle. In a similar way work a row of diagonal cording slanting down to the right, with cord on far left of right-hand triangle as leader, and knotting over it all the cords on right-hand side of work. Now take 2 cords at centre of work through a large china bead. Leave one cord free either side of this centre bead, thread a small bead on each of the next cords. Working down both sides of work, thread a small bead on to every 3rd cord until you reach sides of work. Thread a large bead on to last 2 cords at each side. Return to centre of work. With cord immediately to the left of centre bead as leader work a row of diagonal cording slanting down to the left with all cords on left-hand side of work. Cording should be parallel to previous row worked, and immediately below the small beads to hold them in place. Stop knotting when you reach large bead at side edge (i.e., do not knot cords coming from large bead). Work a similar row of cording down right-hand side.

Work 2 rows of alternate flat [square] knot pattern beneath cording rows just worked (centre knot should use 4 cords in centre of work and be tied immediately below centre large bead to hold it in place).

Leave centre 2 cords free, then using cord on left of centre cords as leader, work a row of diagonal cording slanting down to the left with cords on left-hand side of work. Stop knotting 4 cords from the end.

Still working on these cords only, and working from centre outwards, leave first cord free then thread a small bead on to next and every 3rd cord. Using cord on far right as leader, work a row of diagonal cording below beads, stopping knotting 4 cords from the end.

Work a similar double row of cording with beads between at right-hand side of work.

Tie a flat [square] knot with centre 4 cords, then thread a large bead on to centre 2 cords. Tie a flat [square] knot below bead with centre 4 cords.

Now repeat cording and beaded 'V' pattern just worked but work it in reverse to give a complete centre diamond of cording and beads. In each case leaders for cording rows will be the leaders used before, but with their directions reversed. When final rows of cording have been worked below last row of beads, continue in alternate flat [square] knot pattern. You will need to work left-hand and right-hand sides of work separately to begin with, bringing in 2 cords at inside edge on every row until finally you can work a row straight across all cords.

Continue in alternate flat [square] knot pattern on all cords for a further 2 ins, then repeat cording and beaded diamond. Continue in alternate flat [square] knot pattern as before, until total length of work is approximately 9 ins.

Trim ends to about 1 in.

To make handle

Cut 2 cords, each 6 ft plus 8 times the finished length of handle required (e.g., if you want a finished handle of 2 ft, cut cords 22 ft long). Double cords and place them together on your working surface. Pin by their top loops then tie a flat [square] knot chain with the 4 working ends to a depth of $4\frac{1}{2}$ ins.

Thread a large bead on to 2 centre cords. Work a half knot spiral (first half of the flat [square] knot tied continuously) for about $2\frac{1}{2}$ ins, then thread another large bead on to centre 2 cords. Continue in this way working spirals of half knots with beads threaded on centre cords at $2\frac{1}{2}$ ins intervals, until handle is required length. Tie a flat [square] knot chain for $4\frac{1}{2}$ ins. Trim ends to about 1 in.

To finish

Trim leader cord to about 1 in of knotting. Press ends to back of work, and secure with a few neat stitches. Fold main section in half so each beaded diamond forms central motif on each side of bag. Pin handle in place, so each flat [square] knot section of handle forms one side edge of bag. Stitch firmly in place, pushing cut ends from beginning and end of handle strip to inside of bag.

Press cut ends of main knotted section to inside of purse, and secure with a spot of adhesive.

Tatting

Historical mention of tatting or 'purling' ('pearling') is first made in Chaucer's 'Canterbury Tales', but tatting is known to have been a craft of great accomplishment in Brussels and throughout France and the Near East down the centuries. Known as 'wrap weaving', the craft has flourished in Cambodia. Many beautiful examples of tatting shuttles fashioned in such exotic materials as abalone shell and ivory exist in museum collections throughout Europe and Asia.

Some of the most delightful traditional designs are presented here in their simpler, most effective forms.

Where terminology varies, an equivalent term is given in [ ].

Tatting abbreviations

Laundering tatting

r(s) – *ring(s)*
sr – *small ring*
lr – *large ring*
ds – *double stitch*
p – *picot*
smp – *small picot*
lp – *long picot*
sep – *separated*
cl – *close*
rw – *reverse work*
sp – *space*
ch(s) – *chain(s)*
tog – *together*

* Asterisk
Repeat instructions following the asterisk as many more times as specified in addition to the original.
Repeat instructions in ( ) as many times as specified.

For example, '(R of 8 ds, p, 8 ds, cl) twice', means to make all that is in parentheses twice in all.

Use a warm lather of pure soap flakes and wash in the usual way, either by hand or washing machine. If desired, the article may be spin-dried until it is damp, or left until it is half dry. Place a piece of paper, either plain white or squared, on top of a clean, flat board. Following the correct measurements, draw the shape of the finished article on to the paper, using ruler and set-square for squares and rectangles and a pair of compasses for circles. Using rustless pins, pin the tatting out to the pencilled shape, taking care not to strain the tatting. Pin out the general shape first, then finish by pinning out each picot, loop or space into position. Special points to note carefully when pinning out are:

a When pinning loops, make sure the pin is in the centre of each loop to form balanced lines.

b When pinning scallops, make all the scallops the same size and regularly curved.

c Pull out all picots.

If the tatting requires to be slightly stiffened, use a solution of starch (1 dessertspoonful to 1 pint hot water), and dab lightly over the article. Raise the tatting up off the paper to prevent it sticking as it dries. When dry, remove the pins and press the article lightly with a hot iron.

How to tat

For left-handed pupils

The directions for each stitch apply to both the right and left-handed. The left-handed work from right to left. Place a pocket mirror to the left of each illustration and the exact working position will be reflected.

1

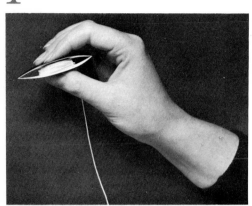

Hold the flat side of the shuttle in a horizontal position, between the thumb and the forefinger of the right hand. Allow approximately 15 ins of the shuttle thread to hang free from the back of the shuttle.

2

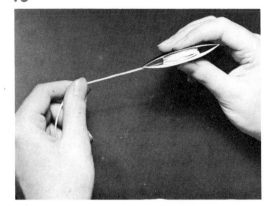

Grasp the free end of the shuttle thread between the thumb and the forefinger of the left hand.

3

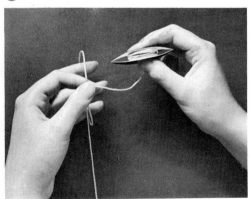

Spread out the middle, ring and little fingers of the left hand and pass the thread over them.

4

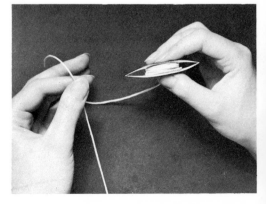

Bring the thread round the fingers of the left hand to form a circle and hold it securely between the thumb and the forefinger.

42

5

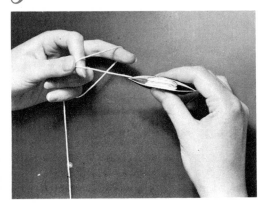

Bend the ring and the little finger of the left hand to catch the thread against the palm.

6

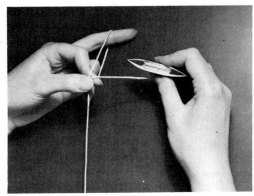

Raise the middle finger of the left hand to 'open' the circle.

7

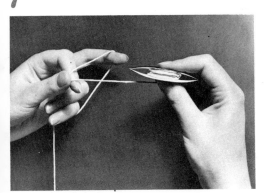

Adjust the thread so that the fingers do not feel strained and draw the shuttle thread out to its full length keeping the right and left hands at equal levels.

8

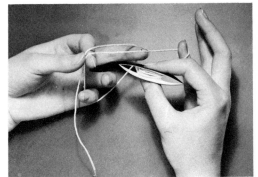

Pass the shuttle thread round the back of the little finger of the right hand. Both hands are now in position to commence the basic stitch in tatting known as the Double Stitch.

First half of double stitch

9

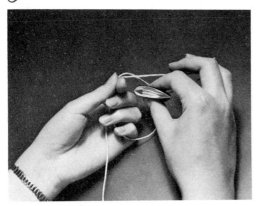

With the thread in position, drop the middle finger of the left hand and move the shuttle forward passing it under the shuttle thread and through the circle.

10

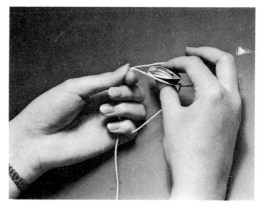

Bring the shuttle back over the circle of thread and under the shuttle thread.

11

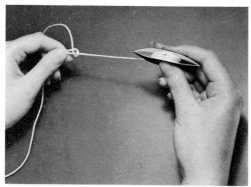

Relaxing the fingers of the left hand, drop the thread from the little finger of the right hand and draw the shuttle thread taut with a sharp jerk.

12

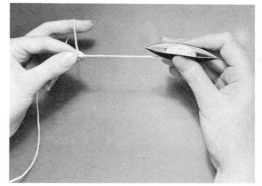

Slowly raise the middle finger of the left hand, slide the loop into position between the thumb and forefinger. This completes the first half of the double stitch.

Second half of double stitch

13

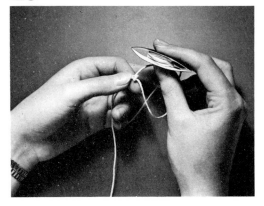

Move the shuttle forward, dropping the shuttle thread and passing the shuttle over the circle and back through between the circle and shuttle threads.

14

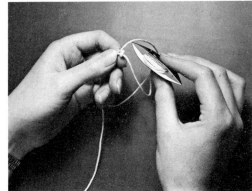

15

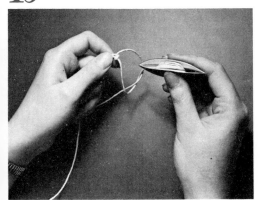

Drop the middle finger of the left hand.

16

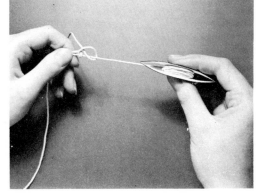

Relaxing the fingers of the left hand, draw the shuttle thread taut with a sharp jerk.

17

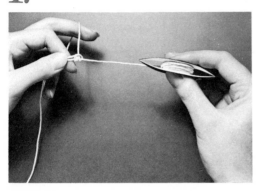

18

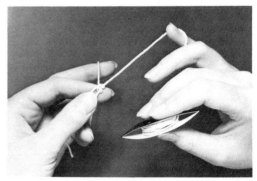

Slowly raise the middle finger of the left hand to slide the loop into position next to the first half of the stitch. This completes the second half of the double stitch.

This shows hands and shuttle in position to commence next double stitch.
Once this stitch has been properly mastered you should be able to work any of the designs in this book.
Practise the following directions. They give in detail the fundamentals of rings, picots and joinings.

Rings, picots and joinings

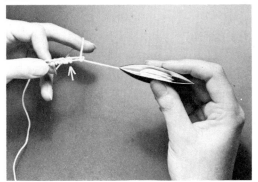

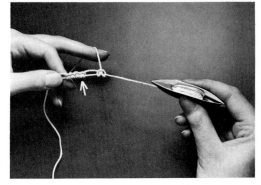

First ring
As each double stitch is formed slide it along the circle of thread to meet the preceding double stitch. Hold them securely between the thumb and forefinger. (See the arrows in *figs 19, 20 and 21.*)
Make four double stitches. Then make the first half of a double stitch sliding it to within $\frac{1}{4}$ in of the preceding stitch.

Now complete the double stitch.

21

Slide the stitch along the ring to meet the first four double stitches. The small loop formed between the last two double stitches is a picot. The size of this may be altered as desired by adjusting the space left from the preceding stitch. Make three more double stitches. Make a second picot and four double stitches. Make a third picot and four double stitches.

22

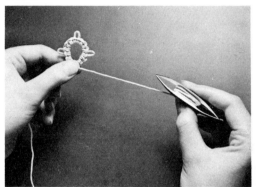

Holding the stitches securely between the thumb and forefinger of the left hand, draw the shuttle thread tight so that the first and last stitches meet forming a ring. In general instructions the ring just completed would be written as:– R of 4 ds, 3 ps sep by 4 ds, 4 ds, cl.

Second ring and joining

23

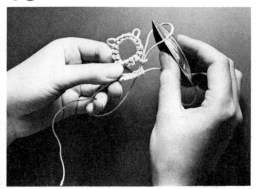

i. Wind the thread round the left hand in position for another ring. Leaving a space of $\frac{1}{4}$ in from base of previous ring, make four double stitches. **ii.** Insert the hook through the last picot of the previous ring and pull the circle thread through, being careful not to twist it as you do so.
iii. Pass the shuttle through the loop. Slowly raise the middle finger of the left hand to draw up the loop. This stands as the first half of the next double stitch.
iv. Now work the **second** half of a double stitch. (A joining and one double stitch have now been completed.) Work 3 ds, 2 ps sep by 4 ds, 4 ds, cl. (Second ring completed.)

Using ball thread and shuttle

The preceding instructions have been given in detail so that you may easily understand the various stages and their abbreviations. Now you are ready to read the same instructions as they will appear later in the book. When your rings are even and your picots uniform in size, proficiency should be acquired in the use of the ball thread and shuttle thread before attempting to follow a full set of instructions. The ball thread is used only in the working of chains. Rings are made with the shuttle thread.

Although some designs are made up of rings and others only contain chains, most designs consist of a combination of these two. For these it is necessary to use the shuttle thread and the ball thread. Commence by tying the ends of the two threads together. Make a ring as before.

24

Unlike rings, chains are made with the thread held across the back of the fingers of the left hand, winding it round the little finger to control the tension.

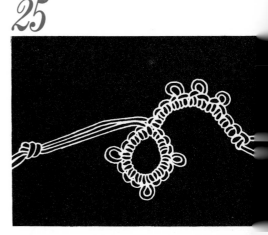

25

A chain consists of a given number of double stitches worked over the ball thread with the shuttle.
A chain may also include picots.

Reversing

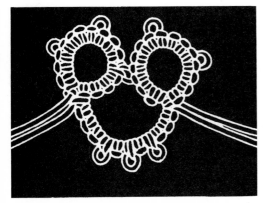

In tatting it will be noticed that the
rounded end of the working ring or chain
faces upwards. When working a design of
rings and chains it is sometimes necessary to reverse work. *(See also fig 27.)*

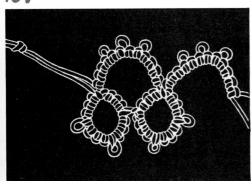

To reverse work turn the ring or chain
just completed to face downwards, i.e., in
the reverse position. The **next** ring or
chain is then worked in the usual way
having the rounded end facing upwards.

Two shuttles

When rings are to be worked in two colours two shuttles are used. The two colours (one in each shuttle) may be alternated. When this takes place the shuttle which made the preceding ring is dropped, the second shuttle is picked up and a ring is made as before. When the rings are separated by a chain, the thread of the second shuttle is held similarly to the ball thread in *fig 24*.

Josephine knot

This is an ornamental ring, consisting of the first half of a double stitch worked a specified number of times.

Further hints

To join threads

(a) When ball and shuttle threads are used, a knot can be avoided at the beginning of the work by filling the shuttle and commencing the ring without cutting the thread.
(b) Make a flat knot, eg, a Reef Knot or a Weaver's Knot close to the base of the last ring or chain. Do not cut off the ends, as the strain during working may loosen the knot.

Finish off ends

28

Make flat knot, eg a Reef Knot or a Weaver's Knot close to the base of the last ring or chain. Do not cut off ends as the strain during working may loosen the knot. With a single strand of Mercer-Crochet Cotton, oversew the ends neatly to the wrong side of the work. *(See fig 28.)*

Equipment

Threads

Coats Mercer-Crochet in no. 10, 20, 40 or
60. All the articles illustrated in this book
can be worked in any of these four sizes.
Note: Coats Mercer-Crochet is available
in a variety of colours in the sizes men-
tioned above. Your retailer will be
pleased to show you our shade card.

Shuttles

Shuttles are made in various materials,
such as bone, tortoiseshell and plastic.
Choose one that is not more than $2\frac{3}{4}$ in
long. A longer shuttle is more clumsy and
makes the speed of work slower. The
designs in this book have been worked
with a Milward tatting shuttle. These
shuttles are supplied in a packet which
contains a separate hook for joinings.

Winding the shuttles

Wind the thread round the centre of the
shuttle. If there is a hole in the centre of
the bobbin, insert the thread through the
hole and tie a knot. Do not wind the thread
beyond the edge of the shuttle. When
making motifs it is advisable to count the
number of turns of thread round the
shuttle so that the amount of thread used
to make one motif can be assessed. This
will prevent unnecessary joining of thread.

Handkerchief edging 1

Materials: Coats Mercer-Crochet no. 40
(20 grms).
1 ball. This model is worked in Dk Jade.
Milward tatting shuttle.
Handkerchief.

Measurements: Depth of edging – ¾ in.

1st row: Tie ball and shuttle threads
together. * R of 8 ds, p, 8 ds, cl, rw. Ch of 5 ds,
p, 5 ds, rw. R of 8 ds, join to p of previous r, 8
ds, cl; repeat from * to next corner. (R of 8 ds,
p, 8 ds, cl) twice; repeat from first * joining
last r to base of first r. Tie ends, cut and oversew neatly on wrong side.

2nd row: Tie ball and shuttle threads
together. Attach shuttle thread to p at join of
first 2 rs, * ch of 10 ds, join by shuttle thread to
p at join of next 2 rs; repeat from * to within
first corner, ch of 10 ds, join by shuttle thread
to next p. Ch of 8 ds, join to p of next corner r.
Ch of 10 ds; repeat from first * joining last ch
by shuttle thread to same place as first ch. Tie
ends, cut and oversew neatly on wrong side.

3rd row: Tie ball and shuttle threads
together. Working over 2nd row attach
shuttle thread to p at join of first 2 rs on 1st
row, * ch of 4 ds, 5 ps sep by 2 ds, 4 ds, working
over 2nd row join by shuttle thread to p at
join of next 2 rs on 1st row; repeat from * to p
of first r at next corner. Ch of 4 ds, 5 ps sep by 2
ds, 4 ds, working over 2nd row join by shuttle
thread to p of next corner r. Ch of 4 ds, 5 ps sep
by 2 ds; repeat from first * joining last ch to
same place as first ch. Tie ends, cut and oversew neatly on wrong side.
Sew edging to handkerchief.
Damp and pin out to measurements.

for colour illustrations, see pages 54 and 55

Handkerchief edging 2

Materials: Coats Mercer-Crochet no. 40
(20 grms).
1 ball. This model is worked in White.
Milward tatting shuttle.
Handkerchief.

Tension (gauge): Depth of edging – $\frac{1}{2}$ in.

1st row: Tie ball and shuttle threads
together. Join to handkerchief $\frac{1}{8}$ in to right of
any corner. * Ch of 4 ds, p, 4 ds, using hook
join by shuttle thread to handkerchief $\frac{1}{4}$ in
along; repeat from * to within $\frac{1}{8}$ in from next
corner. Ch of 5 ds, 3 ps sep by 5 ds, 5 ds, join by
shuttle thread $\frac{1}{8}$ in from corner on next side
(corner ch); repeat from first * 3 times more,
joining last ch to same place as first ch. Tie
ends, cut and oversew neatly on wrong side.

2nd row: Tie ball and shuttle threads
together, join to p of first ch on 1st row. * Ch
of 2 ds, 1 smp, 1 ds, 1 p, 1 ds, 1 lp, 1 ds, 1 p, 1 ds,
1 smp, 2 ds, join by shuttle thread to next p;
repeat from * to within corner ch. Ch of 5 ds,
join by shuttle thread to next p. (Ch of 2 ds,
1 smp, 1 ds, 1 p, 1 ds, 1 lp, 1 ds, 1 p, 1 ds, 1 smp,
2 ds, join by shuttle thread to next p) twice. Ch
of 5 ds, join by shuttle thread to next p; repeat
from first * 3 times more joining last ch to
same place as first ch. Tie ends, cut and oversew neatly on wrong side.
Damp and pin out to measurements.

for colour illustrations, see pages 54 and 55

Handkerchief edging 3

Materials: Coats Mercer-Crochet no. 40
(20 grms).
1 ball. This model is worked in White.
Milward tatting shuttle.
Handkerchief.

Measurements: Depth of edging – $\frac{1}{2}$ in.

1st row: Tie ball and shuttle threads
together. Attach thread to handkerchief $\frac{1}{8}$ in
to right of any corner. * Ch of 4 ds, p, 4 ds,
using hook join by shuttle thread to handker-
chief $\frac{1}{4}$ in along; repeat from * to within $\frac{1}{8}$ in
from next corner. Ch of 5 ds, 3 ps sep by 5 ds,
5 ds, join by shuttle thread $\frac{1}{8}$ in from corner on
next side (corner ch); repeat from first * 3
times more, joining last ch to same place as
first ch. Tie ends, cut and oversew neatly on
wrong side.

2nd row: Tie ball and shuttle threads
together. R of 4 ds, join to first p of first ch,
4 ds, cl, rw. * Ch of 2 ds, 1 p, 1 ds, 1 lp, 1 ds, 1 p,
2 ds, rw. R of 4 ds, join to next p of next ch, 4
ds, cl, rw; repeat from * to within corner ch,
omitting rw at end of last repeat, r of 4 ds, join
to first p of corner ch, 4 ds, cl, rw. Ch of 2 ds,
2 ps sep by 1 ds, 1 ds, 1 lp, 1 ds, 2 ps sep by 1 ds,
2 ds, rw. R of 4 ds, join to next p of corner ch,
4 ds, cl, rw. Ch of 2 ds, 2 ps sep by 1 ds, 1 ds,
1 lp, 1 ds, 2 ps sep by 1 ds, 2 ds, rw. R of 4 ds,
join to next p of corner ch, 4 ds, cl. R of 4 ds,
join to p of next ch, 4 ds, cl, rw; repeat from
first * omitting r at end of last repeat and joining last r to first r. Tie ends, cut and oversew
neatly on wrong side. Damp and pin out to
measurements.

for colour illustrations, see pages 54 and 55

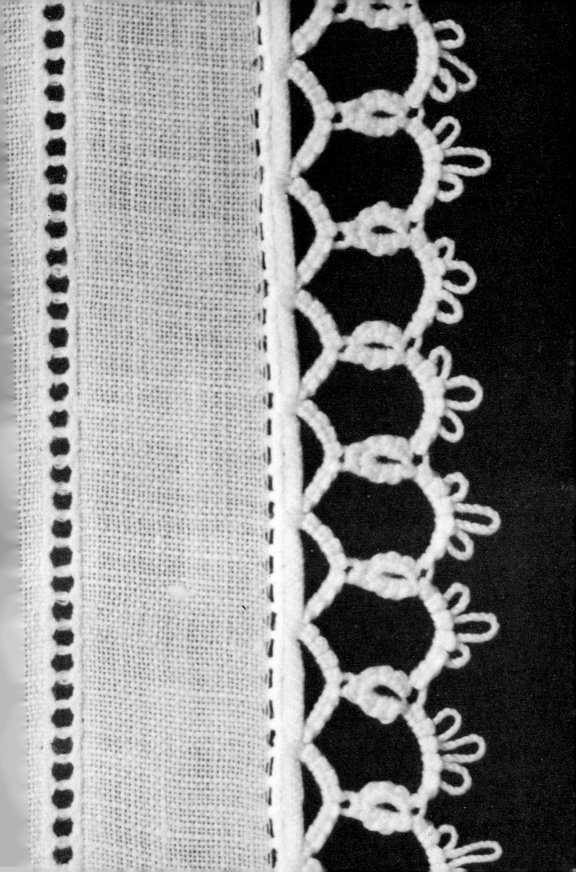

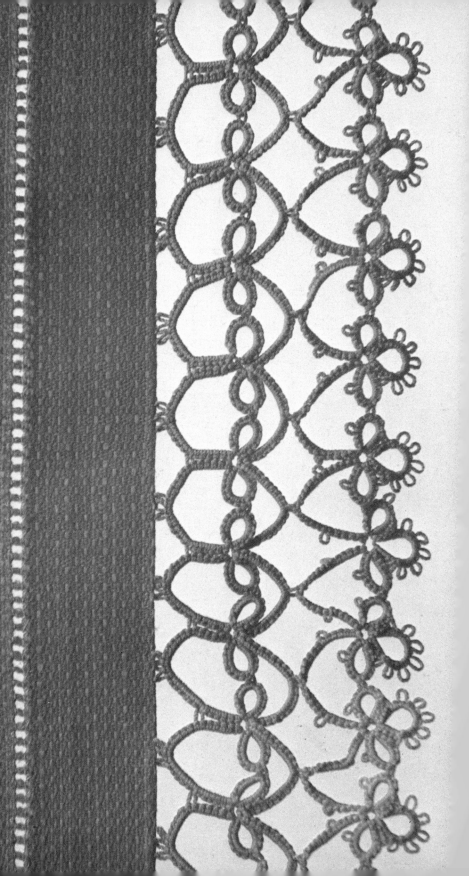

Edging for guest towel

Materials: Coats Mercer-Crochet no. 20
(20 grms).
1 ball. This model is worked in Rose Madder.
Milward tatting shuttle.
Guest towel.
The above quantity is sufficient for 2 edgings.

Measurements:
Depth of edging – 1¾ ins.
Length of edging – 14 ins approximately.

1st row: Tie ball and shuttle threads
together. R of 8 ds, p, 8 ds, cl, rw. Ch of 6 ds, p,
6 ds, 3 ps sep by 1 ds, 6 ds, p, 6 ds, rw. * R of 8
ds, join to p on previous r; 8 ds, cl. R of 8 ds, p,
8 ds, cl, rw. Ch of 6 ds, join by ball thread to
last p on previous ch, 6 ds, 3 ps sep by 1 ds, 6
ds, p, 6 ds, rw; repeat from * 17 times more or
length required, ending with r of 8 ds, join to p
on previous r, 8 ds, cl. Tie ends, cut and oversew neatly on wrong side.

2nd row: Tie ball and shuttle threads
together, attach to base of first r on previous
row. * Ch of 10 ds, p, 10 ds, join by shuttle
thread to base of next 2 rs; repeat from * joining last ch to base of last r on previous row.
Tie ends, cut and oversew neatly on wrong
side.

3rd row: Tie ball and shuttle threads
together. Attach ball thread to p on first ch on
previous row. Ch of 6 ds, p, 6 ds. R of 4 ds, 3 ps
sep by 4 ds, 4 ds, cl. * R of 4 ds, join to last p of
previous r, 2 ds, 6 ps sep by 2 ds, 4 ds, cl R of 4
ds, join to last p on previous r, 4 ds, 2 ps sep by
4 ds, 4 ds, cl. Ch of 6 ds, p, 6 ds, join by shuttle
thread to next p, * * ch of 6 ds, p, 6 ds. R of
4 ds, p, 4 ds, join to centre p on previous r, 4 ds,
p, 4 ds, cl; repeat from * ending last repeat at
* *. Tie ends, cut and oversew neatly on wrong
side.

Damp and pin out to measurements.
Sew neatly to one end of towel.

for colour illustrations, see pages 62 and 63

Motif cheval set

Materials: Coats Mercer-Crochet no. 40
(20 grms).
2 balls. This model is worked in Rose Madder.
Milward tatting shuttle.

Size of motif: 2 ins square.

Measurements: Large mat – 8 × 14 ins.
Small mat – 6 × 8 ins.

Large mat

First motif
1st row: (R of 8 ds, 2 ps sep by 4 ds, 8 ds, cl) 4
times, join to base of first r worked in group.
Sp of ½ in. R of 8 ds, join to corresponding p of
adjacent r, 4 ds, p, 8 ds, cl. (R of 8 ds, 2 ps sep
by 4 ds, 8 ds, cl) twice. R of 8 ds, p, 4 ds, join to
first p of adjacent r in previous group, 8 ds, cl,
join to base of first r worked in group. * Sp of
½ in. R of 8 ds, join to corresponding p of 3rd r
worked in previous group, 4 ds, p, 8 ds, cl. (R of
8 ds, 2 ps sep by 4 ds, 8 ds, cl) twice. R of 8 ds,
p, 4 ds, join to free p of 4th r worked in previous group, 8 ds, cl, join to base of first r
worked in group; repeat from * once more,
joining 3rd and 4th rs to corresponding ps on
previous groups. Sp of ½ in, join to base of first
group of rs worked. Tie ends, cut and oversew
neatly on wrong side.

2nd row: Tie ball and shuttle threads together. Attach thread to first p on any corner r
of first row. * Ch of 2 ds, 3 ps sep by 2 ds, 2 ds. R
of 4 ds, 5 ps sep by 3 ds, 4 ds, cl. Ch of 2 ds, 3 ps
sep by 2 ds, 2 ds, join by shuttle thread to next
p on same r of first row. Ch of 8 ds, join by
shuttle thread to free p on next r of first row.
Ch of 4 ds. R as before. Ch of 4 ds, join by
shuttle thread to next free p on first row. Ch of
8 ds, join by shuttle thread to next p; repeat
from *, joining last ch by shuttle thread to
same place where thread was attached. Tie
ends, cut and oversew neatly on wrong side.

Second motif
Work first row as for first motif.
2nd row: Attach thread and work first ch as
for first motif. R of 4 ds, 3 ps sep by 3 ds, 3 ds,
join to corresponding p on any corner r of first
motif, 3 ds, p, 4 ds, cl. Work to next r as for
first motif. R of 4 ds, 2 ps sep by 3 ds, 3 ds, join
to centre p of corresponding r on first motif, 3
ds, 2 ps sep by 3 ds, 4 ds, cl. Work to next r as
for first motif. R of 4 ds, p, 3 ds, join to corresponding p on next corner r of first motif, 3 ds,
3 ps sep by 3 ds, 4 ds, cl.
Complete as for first motif.
Work 4 rows of 7 motifs, joining adjacent sides
as second motif was joined to first motif.

Small mat *make 2*

Work 3 rows of 4 motifs, joining in same
manner as for large mat.
Damp and press.

Edging for a chairback

Materials: Coats Chain Mercer-Crochet no. 20 (20 grms).

1 ball. This model is worked in Dk Ecru.
Piece of Old Bleach linen, Biscuit, 18 ins. square.
Milward tatting shuttle.

Depth of edging: $3\frac{1}{4}$ ins.

Measurement: $17 \times 20\frac{1}{4}$ ins.
Trim linen to $17\frac{1}{2}$ ins square. Make a $\frac{1}{4}$ in hem all round linen and slip stitch in position.

Edging

1st row: Tie ball and shuttle threads together. * R of 10 ds, 2 ps sep by 4 ds, 10 ds, cl, rw. Ch of 10 ds, 2 ps sep by 4 ds, 10 ds, rw. R of 10 ds, join to last p of previous r, 4 ds, p, 10 ds, cl; repeat from * for length required, having an uneven number of ch scallops. Tie ends, cut and oversew neatly on wrong side.

2nd row: Tie ball and shuttle threads together. R of 10 ds, 2 ps sep by 4 ds, 10 ds, cl, rw. Ch of 10 ds, join to first p on first ch of previous row, 4 ds, join to next p, 10 ds, rw, complete row as for first row, joining each ch to ch of first row. Tie ends, cut and oversew neatly on wrong side.

3rd row: Tie ball and shuttle threads together. R of 10 ds, join to free p on first r of previous row, 4 ds, p, 10 ds, cl, rw. * Ch of 5 ds, 2 ps sep by 12 ds, 5 ds, rw. R of 10 ds, join to last p of previous r, 4 ds, join to next free p on previous row, 10 ds, cl. R of 10 ds, join to next free p on previous row, 4 ds, p, 10 ds, cl, rw; repeat from * omitting r at end of last repeat. Tie ends, cut and oversew neatly on wrong side.

4th row: Tie ball and shuttle threads together. R of 12 ds, join to first p on first ch of previous row, 8 ds, p, 4 ds, cl, rw. * Ch of 14 ds, rw. R of 8 ds, join to last p of previous r, 8 ds, 2 ps sep by 4 ds, 4 ds, cl, rw. Ch of 4 ds, 4 ps sep by 2 ds, 4 ds, rw. R of 10 ds, join to last p of previous r, 4 ds, p, 10 ds, cl, rw. Ch of 4 ds, 4 ps sep by 2 ds, 4 ds, rw. R of 4 ds, join to last p of previous r, 4 ds, join to free p of 2nd r of group, 8 ds, p, 8 ds, cl, rw. Ch of 14 ds, rw. R of 4 ds, join to last p of previous r, 8 ds, join to next free p on previous row, 4 ds, join to next free p, 8 ds, cl, rw. Ch of 2 ds, 3 ps sep by 2 ds, 2 ds, rw. R of 8 ds, join to next free p on previous row, 4 ds, join to next free p, 8 ds, p, 4 ds, cl, rw; repeat from * omitting ch and r at end of last repeat and omitting last p of last r worked. Tie ends, cut and oversew neatly on wrong side.
Sew edging to one end of linen.
Damp and press.

for colour illustration, see page 70

Edgings for trolley cloths

Materials: Coats Mercer-Crochet no. 20 (20 grms).
3 balls. This model is worked in Coral Pink. Milward tatting shuttle.
¾ yd fine Pink linen, 36 ins wide, to match or tone.
The above quantity is sufficient for 2 trolley cloths.

Depth of edging: 1¼ ins.

Measurements: 16 × 24 ins.

Suitable fabric brand: Old Bleach linen C15 (Rose).

1st row: Tie ball and shuttle threads together. * R of 3 ds, 3 ps sep by 3 ds, 3 ds, cl, rw. Ch of 12 ds, p, 12 ds, rw. R of 3 ds, p, 3 ds, join to centre p of previous r, 3 ds, p, 3 ds, cl; repeat from * 25 times more or length required to next corner. R of 3 ds, 3 ps sep by 3 ds, 3 ds, cl, rw. Ch of 12 ds, p, 8 ds, join by shuttle thread to centre p of previous r, 8 ds, p, 12 ds, rw. R of 3 ds, p, 3 ds, join to same p as last joining, 3 ds, p, 3 ds, cl. * * R of 3 ds, 3 ps sep by 3 ds, 3 ds, cl, rw. Ch of 12 ds, p, 12 ds, rw. R of 3 ds, p, 3 ds, join to centre p of previous r, 3 ds, p, 3 ds, cl; repeat from * * 38 times more or length required to next corner. R of 3 ds, 3 ps sep by 3 ds, 3 ds, cl, rw. Ch of 12 ds, p, 8 ds, join by shuttle thread to centre p of previous r, 8 ds, p, 12 ds, rw. R of 3 ds, p, 3 ds, join to same p as last joining, 3 ds, p, 3 ds, cl; repeat from first * once more, join to base of first r. Tie ends, cut and oversew neatly on wrong side.

2nd row: Tie ball and shuttle threads together. Attach thread to p of first ch. * R of 12 ds, join to p of next ch, 12 ds, cl, rw. Ch of 6 ds, 5 ps sep by 2 ds, 6 ds, join to same p as last joining, rw; repeat from * along side. R of 8 ds, p, 8 ds, cl, rw. Ch of 4 ds, 5 ps sep by 2 ds, 4 ds, join by shuttle thread to p of previous r, rw. R of 8 ds, join to p of next ch, 8 ds, cl, rw. Ch of 4 ds, 5 ps sep by 2 ds, 4 ds, join by shuttle thread to same p as last joining, rw; repeat from first * ending with r of 12 ds, join to same p as first joining. 12 ds, cl, rw. Ch of 6 ds, 5 ps sep by 2 ds, 6 ds, join to same p as last joining. Tie ends, cut and oversew neatly on wrong side.
Damp and pin out to measurements.

To make up

Cut 2 pieces of linen 15 × 23 ins. Turn back ½ ir hem, mitre corners and slip stitch in position, or mount as desired.
Sew edging neatly to edge of fabric.

for colour illustration, see page 71

Doily

Materials: Coats Mercer-Crochet no. 20 (20 grms).
1 ball.
This model is worked in Lt. French Blue.
Milward tatting shuttle.

Tension (gauge): First 2 rows = 1 in diameter.

Measurements: 9½ ins from point to point.

1st row: R of 2 ds, 6 ps sep by 4 ds, 2 ds, cl. Tie ends, cut and oversew neatly on wrong side.

2nd row: Tie ball and shuttle threads together. R of 4 ds, join to any p on previous row, 4 ds, cl, rw. * Ch of 4 ds, 2 ps sep by 4 ds, 4 ds, rw. R of 4 ds, join to next p on previous row, 4 ds, cl, rw; repeat from * omitting a r at end of last repeat and joining last ch to base of first r. Tie ends, cut and oversew neatly on wrong side.

3rd row: Tie ball and shuttle threads together. Attach thread to first p on any ch on previous row, * ch of 3 ds, p, 3 ds, join by shuttle thread to next p, ch of 3 ds, 2 ps sep by 3 ds, 3 ds, join by shuttle thread to next p; repeat from * joining last ch to same place as join. Tie ends, cut and oversew neatly on wrong side.

4th row: Tie ball and shuttle threads together. Attach thread to single p on small ch of previous row, * ch of 4 ds, p, 4 ds, join by shuttle thread to first p on next ch, ch of 4 ds, join by shuttle thread to second p on same ch, ch of 4 ds, p, 4 ds, join by shuttle thread to p on next ch; repeat from * joining last ch to same p as join. Tie ends, cut and oversew neatly on wrong side.

for detail, see page 77

5th row: Tie ball and shuttle threads together. R of 4 ds, join to first p on previous row, 4 ds, cl, rw, * Ch of 5 ds, p, 5 ds, rw. R of 4 ds, join to next p, 4 ds, cl, rw. Ch of 5 ds, 3 ps sep by 5 ds, 5 ds, rw. * * R of 4 ds, join to next p, 4 ds, cl, rw; repeat from * ending last repeat at * * joining last ch to base of first r. Tie ends, cut and oversew neatly on wrong side.

6th row: Tie ball and shuttle threads together. Attach thread to first p on previous row. * Ch of 3 ds, 2 ps sep by 3 ds, 3 ds, join by shuttle thread to next p, (ch of 3 ds, p, 3 ds, join by shuttle thread to next p) twice, ch of 3 ds, 2 ps sep by 3 ds, 3 ds, join by shuttle thread to next p; repeat from * joining last ch to same place as join. Tie ends, cut and oversew neatly on wrong side.

7th row: Tie ball and shuttle threads together. Attach thread to first p on previous row. * Ch of 2 ds, p, 2 ds, join by shuttle thread to next p, ch of 3 ds, p, 3 ds, join by shuttle thread to next p, ch of 4 ds, p, 4 ds, join by shuttle thread to next p, ch of 3 ds, p, 3 ds, join by shuttle thread to next p, ch of 2 ds, p, 2 ds, join by shuttle thread to next p, ch of 3 ds, p, 3 ds, join by shuttle thread to next p; repeat from * joining last ch to first p. Tie ends, cut and oversew neatly on wrong side.

8th row: Tie ball and shuttle threads together. R of 4 ds, p, 4 ds, join to p of large ch on previous row, 4 ds, p, 4 ds, cl, rw. * Ch of 3 ds, 4 ps sep by 3 ds, 3 ds, rw. (R of 4 ds, join to next p, 4 ds, cl, rw. Ch of 3 ds, p, 3 ds, rw) 4 times. R of 4 ds, join to next p, 4 ds, cl, rw. Ch of 3 ds, 4 ps sep by 3 ds, 3 ds, * * rw. R of 4 ds, p, 4 ds, join to next p, 4 ds, p, 4 ds, cl, rw; repeat from * ending last repeat at * * and joining last ch by shuttle thread to base of first r. Tie ends, cut and oversew neatly on wrong side.

9th row: Tie ball and shuttle threads together. R of 4 ds, join to second p on first large ch on previous row, 4 ds, cl, rw. * Ch of 3 ds, 3 ps sep by 3 ds, 3 ds, rw. R of 4 ds, miss 1 p, join to next p, 4 ds, join to next p, 4 ds, cl, rw. Ch of 3 ds, 7 ps sep by 3 ds, 3 ds, rw. R of 4 ds, miss 2 ps, join to next p, 4 ds, join to next p, 4 ds, cl, rw. Ch of 3 ds, 3 ps sep by 3 ds, 3 ds, rw. R of 4 ds, miss 1 p, join to next p, 4 ds, cl, rw. Ch of 3 ds, 3 ps sep by 3 ds, 3 ds, rw. * * R of 4 ds, miss 2 ps, join to next p, 4 ds, cl, rw; repeat from * ending last repeat at * * and joining last ch to base of first r. Tie ends, cut and oversew neatly on wrong side.

10th row: Tie ball and shuttle threads together. Attach thread to first p on large ch of previous row. * Ch of 2 ds, p, 4 ds, p, 2 ds, miss 1 p, join by shuttle thread to next p; repeat from * joining last ch to same place as join. Tie ends, cut and oversew ends neatly on wrong side.

11th row: Tie ball and shuttle threads together. Attach thread to first and last p of previous row. * (Ch of 2 ds, p, 2 ds, join by shuttle thread to next p) 4 times, ch of 2 ds, p, 2 ds, join by shuttle thread to next 2 ps, (ch of 2 ds, p, 2 ds, join by shuttle thread to next p) 8 times, ch of 2 ds, p, 2 ds, * * join by shuttle thread to next 2 ps; repeat from * ending last repeat at * * and joining last ch to same place as first ch. Tie ends, cut and oversew neatly on wrong side.

12th row: Tie ball and shuttle threads together. Attach thread to first and last p of previous row. * (Ch of 3 ds, p, 3 ds, join by shuttle thread to next p) 3 times, ch of 3 ds, p, 3 ds, join by shuttle thread to next 2 ps, (ch of 3 ds, p, 3 ds, join by shuttle thread to next p) 7 times, ch of 3 ds, p, 3 ds, * * join by shuttle thread to next 2 ps; repeat from * ending last repeat at * * and joining last ch to first ch. Tie ends, cut and oversew neatly on wrong side.

13th row: Tie ball and shuttle threads together. R of 4 ds, p, 4 ds, join to first p on previous row, 4 ds, join to next p, 4 ds, p, 4 ds, cl, rw. * Ch of 3 ds, 9 ps sep by 3 ds, 3 ds, rw. * * R of 4 ds, p, 4 ds, miss 2 ps, join to next p, 4 ds, join to next p, 4 ds, p, 4 ds, cl, rw; repeat from * ending last repeat at * * and joining last ch to base of first r. Tie ends, cut and oversew neatly on wrong side.

14th row: Tie ball and shuttle threads together. Attach thread to second p on first ch of previous row. * (Ch of 4 ds, 2 ps sep by 4 ds, 4 ds, miss 2 ps, join by shuttle thread to next p) twice, ch of 4 ds, p, 4 ds, miss 2 ps, join by shuttle thread to next p; repeat from * joining last ch by shuttle thread to first ch. Tie ends, cut and oversew neatly on wrong side.

15th row: Tie ball and shuttle threads together. R of 4 ds, p, 4 ds, join to first single p on first small ch of previous row, 4 ds, p, 4 ds, cl, rw. * Ch of 4 ds, 3 ps sep by 4 ds, 4 ds, join by shuttle thread to next p, (ch of 2 ds, p, 2 ds, join by shuttle thread to next p, ch of 3 ds, p, 3 ds, join by shuttle thread to next p) 6 times, ch of 2 ds, p, 2 ds, join by shuttle thread to next p, ch of 4 ds, 3 ps sep by 4 ds, 4 ds, rw. * * R of 4 ds, p, 4 ds, join to next p, 4 ds, p, 4 ds, cl, rw; repeat from * ending last repeat at * * joining

last ch to base of first r. Tie ends, cut and oversew neatly on wrong side.

16th row: Tie ball and shuttle threads together. R of 4 ds, join to first p on first ch of previous row, 4 ds, cl, rw. (Ch of 4 ds, p, 4 ds, rw. R of 4 ds, join to next p, 4 ds, cl, rw) twice. * Ch of 4 ds, p, 4 ds, rw. R of 4 ds, miss next p, join to next p, 4 ds, cl, rw. (Ch of 2 ds, p, 2 ds, rw. R of 4 ds, join to next p, 4 ds, cl, rw) 10 times. Ch of 4 ds, p, 4 ds, rw. R of 4 ds, miss next p, join to next p, 4 ds, cl, rw. (Ch of 4 ds, p, 4 ds, rw. R of 4 ds, join to next p, 4 ds, cl, rw) 5 times; repeat from * ending last repeat with (ch of 4 ds, p, 4 ds, rw. R of 4 ds, join to next p, 4 ds, cl, rw) twice. Ch of 4 ds, p, 4 ds, join by shuttle thread to base of first r. Tie ends, cut and oversew neatly on wrong side.

17th row: Tie ball and shuttle threads together. Attach thread to p on first ch of previous row. (Ch of 5 ds, p, 5 ds, join by shuttle thread to next p) twice. * (Ch of 2 ds, p, 2 ds, join by shuttle thread to next p) 3 times. (Ch of 3 ds, p, 3 ds, join by shuttle thread to next p) 5 times. (Ch of 2 ds, p, 2 ds, join by shuttle thread to next p) 3 times. * * (Ch of 5 ds, p, 5 ds, join by shuttle thread to next p) 6 times; repeat from * ending last repeat at * *. (Ch of 5 ds, p, 5 ds, join by shuttle thread to next p) 4 times, joining last ch to same place as first ch. Tie ends, cut and oversew neatly on wrong side.

Damp and pin out to measurements.

Runner

Materials: Coats Mercer-Crochet no. 10
(20 grms).
3 balls. This model is worked in Spring Green.
Milward tatting shuttle.

Measurements: 36 × 8½ ins.

1st row: Tie ball and shuttle threads together. Lr of 4 ds, 8 ps sep by 3 ds, 4 ds, cl. Rw, ch of 6 ds, p, 6 ds. Rw, r of 10 ds, p, 3 ds, p, 7 ds, cl. Rw, ch of 6 ds, 5 ps sep by 3 ds, 4 ds. Rw, r of 9 ds, join to last p of previous r, 9 ds, p, 3 ds, cl. * Lr of 3 ds, join to p of previous r, 6 ds, 3 ps sep by 3 ds, 2 ds, 3 ps sep by 3 ds, 6 ds, p, 3 ds, cl. R of 3 ds, join to last p of lr, 9 ds, p, 9 ds, cl. Rw, ch of 4 ds, 8 ps sep by 3 ds, 4 ds. Rw, r of 9 ds, join to p of last r, 9 ds, p, 3 ds, cl; repeat from * 23 times more, lr of 3 ds, join to p of previous r, 6 ds, 3 ps sep by 3 ds, 2 ds, 3 ps sep by 3 ds, 6 ds, p, 3 ds, cl. R of 3 ds, join to last p of lr, 9 ds, p, 9 ds, cl. Rw, ch of 4 ds, 5 ps sep by 3 ds, 6 ds. Rw, r of 7 ds, join to p of previous r, 3 ds, p, 10 ds, cl. Rw, ch of 6 ds, p, 6 ds. Rw, lr of 4 ds, 8 ps sep by 3 ds, 4 ds, cl. Rw, ch of 6 ds, join to p of previous ch, 6 ds. Rw, r of 10 ds, p, 3 ds, p, 7 ds, cl. Rw, ch of 6 ds, join to first p of adjoining ch, (3 ds, join to next p of same ch) twice, 3 ds, 2 ps sep by 3 ds, 4 ds. Rw, r of 9 ds, join to last p of previous r, 9 ds, p, 3 ds, cl. * Lr of 3 ds, join to p of previous r, 6 ds, 3 ps sep by 3 ds, 2 ds, 3 ps sep by 3 ds, 6 ds, p, 3 ds, cl. R of 3 ds, join to last p of lr, 9 ds, p, 9 ds, cl. Rw, ch of 4 ds, 2 ps sep by 3 ds, 3 ds, join to 3rd p of adjacent ch, (3 ds, join to next p of same ch 3 times, 3 ds, 2 ps sep by 3 ds, 4 ds. Rw, r of 9 ds, join to p of previous r, 9 ds, p, 3 ds, cl; repeat from last * 23 times more, lr of 3 ds, join to p of previous r, 6 ds, 3 ps sep by 3 ds, 2 ds, 3 ps sep by 3 ds, 6 ds, p, 3 ds, cl. R of 3 ds, join to last p of lr, 9 ds, p, 9 ds, cl. Rw, ch of 4 ds, 2 ps sep by 3 ds, 3 ds, join to 3rd p of adjacent ch, (3 ds, join to next p of same ch) twice, 6 ds. Rw, r of 7 ds, join to p

for colour illustration, see page 79

of previous r, 3 ds, p, 10 ds, cl. Rw, ch of 6 ds, join to p of adjacent ch, 6 ds, join to base of first lr. Tie ends, cut and oversew neatly on wrong side.

2nd row: Tie ball and shuttle threads together. R of 11 ds, 2 ps sep by 11 ds, 3 ds, cl. Lr of 3 ds, join to last p of previous r, 3 ds, 3 ps sep by 3 ds, 3 ds, join to 5th p of first lr of first row, 3 ds, 3 ps sep by 3 ds, 3 ds, cl. R of 3 ds, join to last p of lr, 11 ds, p, 11 ds, cl. Rw, ch of 4 ds, 8 ps sep by 3 ds, 4 ds. Rw, r of 11 ds, join to p of previous r, 11 ds, p, 3 ds, cl. Lr of 3 ds, join to p of previous r, 6 ds, 2 ps sep by 3 ds, 3 ds, join to p of next r on first row, 3 ds, 2 ps sep by 3 ds, 6 ds, p, 3 ds, cl. R of 3 ds, join to last p of last lr, 11 ds, p, 11 ds, cl. * Rw, ch of 4 ds, 8 ps sep by 3 ds, 4 ds. Rw, r of 11 ds, join to p of previous r, 11 ds, p, 3 ds, cl. Lr of 3 ds, join to p of previous r, 6 ds, 2 ps sep by 3 ds, 3 ds, join to 3rd p of lr of first row, 2 ds, join to next p of same lr, 3 ds, 2 ps sep by 3 ds, 6 ds, p, 3 ds, cl. R of 3 ds, join to last p of lr, 11 ds, p, 11 ds, cl; repeat from * 24 times more. Rw, ch of 4 ds, 8 ps sep by 3 ds, 4 ds. Rw, r of 11 ds, join to p of previous r, 11 ds, p, 3 ds, cl. Lr of 3 ds, join to p of previous r, 6 ds, 2 ps sep by 3 ds, 3 ds, join to p of single r on first row, 3 ds, 2 ps sep by 3 ds, 6 ds, p, 3 ds, cl. R of 3 ds, join to last p of last lr, 11 ds, p, 11 ds, cl. Rw, ch of 4 ds, 8 ps sep by 3 ds, 4 ds. Rw, r of 11 ds, join to p of last r, 11 ds, p, 3 ds, cl. Lr of 3 ds, join to p of last r, 3 ds, 2 ps sep by 3 ds, 3 ds, join to 4th p of end r, 3 ds, 4 ps sep by 3 ds, 3 ds, cl. R of 3 ds, join to last p of lr, 11 ds, p, 11 ds, cl. Rw, ch of 4 ds, 8 ps sep by 3

ds, 4 ds, Rw, r of 9 ds, join to p of last r, 9 ds, p, 3 ds, cl. R of 3 ds, join to p of last r, 9 ds, p, 9 ds, cl. Rw, ch of 4 ds, 8 ps sep by 3 ds, 4 ds. Rw, r of 11 ds, join to p of last r, 11 ds, p, 3 ds, cl. Lr of 3 ds, join to p of last r, 3 ds, 2 ps sep by 3 ds, 3 ds, miss 2 ps on last lr, join to next p, 3 ds, join to next p on end r, 3 ds, 3 ps sep by 3 ds, 3 ds, cl. R of 3 ds, join to last p of lr, 11 ds, p, 11 ds, cl. Now work along other side to correspond, joining last lr and last r to adjacent ps and last ch to base of first lr. Tie ends, cut and oversew neatly on wrong side.

3rd row: Tie ball and shuttle threads together. R of 6 ds, join to last p of ch before double rings at one end of runner, 4 ds, join to first p of next ch, 6 ds, cl. Rw, ch of 4 ds, 6 ps sep by 4 ds, 4 ds, join by shuttle thread to next p of same ch, ch of 4 ds, join to first p of adjacent ch, 4 ds, join to next p of same ch, 4 ds, 5 ps sep by 4 ds, 4 ds, miss 2 ps of ch on second row, join by shuttle thread to next p of same ch, * ch of 4 ds, join to first p of adjacent ch, 4 ds, join to next p of same ch, 4 ds, 6 ps sep by 4 ds, 4 ds, join by shuttle thread to last p of ch on second row, ch of 3 ds, join by shuttle thread to first p of next ch on second row, 4 ds, join to first p of adjacent ch, (4 ds, join to next p on same ch) twice, 4 ds, 5 ps sep by 4 ds, 4 ds, miss 2 ps of ch on second row, join by shuttle thread to next p on same ch, 3 ds, join by shuttle thread to next p of same ch; repeat from * until 2 centre ps of second last ch of this side have been joined, 4 ds, join to first p of adjacent ch, 4 ds, join to next p of same ch, 4 ds, 6 ps sep by 4 ds, miss 2 ps of ch on second row, join by shuttle thread to next p of same ch, 3 ds, join by shuttle thread to first p of next ch on second row, 4 ds, join to first p of adjacent ch, (4 ds, join to next p on same ch) twice, (4 ds, 5 ps sep by 4 ds, 4 ds, miss 2 ps of ch on second row, join by shuttle thread to next p on same ch, 4 ds, join to first p of adjacent ch, 4 ds, join to next p on same ch) twice, 4 ds, 4 ps sep by 4 ds, 4 ds. Rw, r of 6 ds, join to last p of same ch on second row, 4 ds, join to first p of next ch, 6 ds, cl. Rw, ch of 4 ds, join to first p of adjacent ch, 4 ds, 5 ps sep by 4 ds, 4 ds. Now continue to work other side to correspond joining last ch to first p of first ch and last ch to base of first r. Tie ends, cut and oversew neatly on wrong side.

4th row: Tie ball and shuttle threads to centre p of any ch on third row, ch of 3 ds, 6 ps sep by 3 ds, 3 ds, * join by shuttle thread to centre p of next ch, 3 ds, join to first p of adjacent ch, 3 ds, 5 ps sep by 3 ds, 3 ds; repeat from * all round, joining last ch to first p of first ch and joining last ch to same p as threads were joined. Tie ends, cut and oversew neatly on wrong side.

Damp and pin out to measurements.

Lemonade set

Materials: Coats Mercer-Crochet no. 20
(20 grms).
2 balls. This model is worked in Jade.
Milward tatting shuttle.
1 piece of glass 6½ ins diameter.
4 pieces of glass 4 ins diameter.
The above quantity is sufficient for 1 large mat
and 4 glass mats.

Measurements:
Large mat – 6½ ins diameter approximately.
Glass mat – 4 ins diameter approximately.

Large mat

1st row: Tie ball and shuttle threads together. R of 3 ds, 5 ps sep by 3 ds, 3 ds, cl, rw. *
Ch of 4 ds, 3 ps sep by 4 ds, 4 ds, rw. R of 3 ds, p,
3 ds, join to second last p on previous r, 3 ds,
3 ps sep by 3 ds, 3 ds, cl, rw; repeat from * 8
times more, joining second last p on last r to
second p on first r. Ch of 4 ds, 3 ps sep by 4 ds,
4 ds, join by shuttle thread to base of first r.
Tie ends, cut and oversew neatly on wrong
side.

2nd row: Tie ball and shuttle threads
together. Attach thread to centre p of any ch
on previous row. * Ch of 8 ds, p, 8 ds, join by
shuttle thread to centre p on next ch; repeat
from * joining last ch to same place as first ch.
Tie ends, cut and oversew neatly on wrong
side.

3rd row: Tie ball and shuttle threads
together. R of 12 ds, join to p of any ch on previous row, 12 ds, cl, rw. * Ch of 12 ds, p, 5 ds,
join by shuttle thread to same place as chs on
previous row. Ch of 5 ds, join by ball thread to
p on previous ch, 12 ds, * * rw. R of 12 ds, join
to next p on previous row, 12 ds, cl, rw; repeat
from * ending last repeat at * *, join last ch by
ball thread to base of first r. Do not tie ends.

4th row: Ch of 8 ds, 5 ps sep by 4 ds, 6 ds, p,
8 ds, join by shuttle thread to joining of chs on
previous row. Ch of 8 ds, join by ball thread to
adjacent p on previous ch, 6 ds, join by ball
thread to adjacent p on previous ch, 4 ds, 4 ps
sep by 4 ds, 8 ds, join by shuttle thread to base
of next r. * * Ch of 8 ds, join by ball thread to
last p on previous ch, 4 ds, 4 ps sep by 4 ds,
6 ds, p, 8 ds, join by shuttle thread to joining of
chs on previous row; repeat from * ending last
repeat at * * joining p of last ch to p of first ch
to correspond and last ch to base of first ch.

for colour illustration, see page 83

Tie ends, cut and oversew neatly on wrong side.

5th row: Tie ball and shuttle threads together. R of 5 ds, 3 ps sep by 1 ds, 5 ds, join to any p to left of any join, 5 ds, join to next p on next ch, 5 ds, 3 ps sep by 1 ds, 5 ds, cl, rw. * Ch of 4 ds, 4 ps sep by 4 ds, 4 ds, rw. R of 5 ds, 3 ps sep by 1 ds, 5 ds, miss next p on same ch, join to next p, 5 ds, join to next p on next ch, 5 ds, 3 ps sep by 1 ds, 5 ds, cl, rw; repeat from * omitting r at end of last repeat and joining last ch by shuttle thread to base of first r. Do not tie ends.

6th row: Ch of 8 ds, p, 6 ds, 3 ps sep by 4 ds, 4 ds, rw. R of 5 ds, 3 ps sep by 1 ds, 5 ds, join to second p on next ch, 5 ds, join to next p on same ch, 5 ds, 3 ps sep by 1 ds, 5 ds, cl, rw. * Ch of 4 ds, 3 ps sep by 4 ds, 6 ds, p, 8 ds, join by shuttle thread to base of next r. Ch of 8 ds, join by ball thread to last p on previous ch, 6 ds, join by ball thread to adjacent p on previous ch, 4 ds, 2 ps sep by 4 ds, 4 ds, rw. R of 5 ds, 3 ps sep by 1 ds, 5 ds, miss 1 p of next ch, join to next p, 5 ds, join to next p, 5 ds, 3 ps sep by 1 ds, 5 ds, cl, rw; repeat from * ending with ch of 4 ds, 2 ps sep by 4 ds, 4 ds, join to next p on first ch, 6 ds, join to next p on first ch, 8 ds, join to base of next r. Tie ends, cut and oversew neatly on wrong side.

7th row: Lr of 8 ds, p, 8 ds, join to p at left of any join, 5 ds, join to next p, 8 ds, p, 8 ds, cl, rw. Leave a sp of $\frac{3}{8}$ in. R of 4 ds, 3 ps sep by 4 ds, 4 ds, cl, rw. * Leave a sp of $\frac{3}{8}$ in. Lr of 8 ds, join to last p on previous lr, 8 ds, join to next p on previous row, 5 ds, join to next p, 8 ds, p, 8 ds, cl, rw. Leave a sp of $\frac{3}{8}$ in. R of 4 ds, join to last p on previous r, 4 ds, 2 ps sep by 4 ds, 4 ds, cl, rw; repeat from * joining last lr to first lr and

last r to first r. Tie ends, cut and oversew neatly on wrong side.

Glass mat *make 4*

Work as large mat for 3 rows. Do not tie ends.

4th row: * Ch of 4 ds, 3 ps sep by 4 ds, 4 ds, join by shuttle thread to joining of chs on previous row. Ch of 4 ds, 3 ps sep by 4 ds, 4 ds, join by shuttle thread to base of next r; repeat from * joining last ch to base of first ch. Tie ends, cut and oversew neatly on wrong side.

5th row: Lr of 8 ds, p, 8 ds, join to centre p of any ch on previous row, 8 ds, p, 8 ds, cl, rw. Leave a sp of $\frac{3}{8}$ in. R of 4 ds, 3 ps sep by 4 ds, 4 ds, cl, rw. * Leave a sp of $\frac{3}{8}$ in. Lr of 8 ds, join to last p on previous lr, 8 ds, join to centre p of next ch on previous row, 8 ds, p, 8 ds, cl, rw. Leave a sp of $\frac{3}{8}$ in. R of 4 ds, join to last p on previous r, 4 ds, 2 ps sep by 4 ds, 4 ds, cl, rw; repeat from * joining last p of last lr to first p of first lr and last p of last r to first p of first r. Tie ends, cut and oversew neatly on wrong side.

Damp and pin out to measurements. Slip over glass.

Motif coffee table mat

Materials: Coats Mercer-Crochet no. 20
(20 grms).
3 balls. This model is worked in Emerald
Green.
Milward tatting shuttle.

Size of motif: 3 ins.

Measurements: 21 × 18 ins.

First motif

1st row: R of 3 ds, 3 ps sep by 3 ds, 3 ds, cl.
* Sp of ¼ in. R of 3 ds, join to last p of previous
r, 3 ds, 2 ps sep by 3 ds, 3 ds, cl; repeat from * 4
times more, joining last p of last r to first p of
first r. Tie ends, cut and oversew neatly on
wrong side.

2nd row: Tie ball and shuttle threads
together. Sr of 4 ds, 2 ps sep by 4 ds, 4 ds, cl, rw.
Ch of 9 ds, join to any p on previous row, 9 ds,

rw. * Sr of 4 ds, join to last p on previous sr,
4 ds, p, 4 ds, cl, rw. Ch of 5 ds, p, 5 ds, rw. R of
3 ds, join to last p on previous sr, 3 ds, 2 ps sep
by 3 ds, 3 ds, cl, rw. Ch of 3 ds, rw. Lr of 3 ds,
join to last p on previous r, 2 ds, 2 ps sep by
2 ds, 2 ds, lp, 2 ds, 3 ps sep by 2 ds, 3 ds, cl, rw.
Ch of 3 ds, rw. R of 3 ds, join to last p on previous lr, 3 ds, 2 ps sep by 3 ds, 3 ds, cl, rw. Ch of
5 ds, join to p on corresponding ch, 5 ds, rw.
* * Sr of 4 ds, join to last p on previous r, 4 ds,
p, 4 ds, cl, rw. Ch of 9 ds, join to next p on previous row, 9 ds, rw; repeat from * ending last
repeat at * * joining last r to first sr, p of last
ch to p of first ch and last ch to base of first r.
Tie ends, cut and oversew neatly on wrong
side.

Second motif

Work as first motif for 1 row.

2nd row: Tie ball and shuttle threads
together. Sr of 4 ds, 2 ps sep by 4 ds, 4 ds, cl,
rw. Ch of 9 ds, join to any p on previous row,
9 ds, rw. Sr of 4 ds, join to last p on previous sr,
4 ds, p, 4 ds, cl, rw. Ch of 5 ds, p, 5 ds, rw. R of
3 ds, join to last p on previous sr, 3 ds, 2 ps sep
by 3 ds, 3 ds, cl, rw. Ch of 3 ds, rw. Lr of 3 ds,
join to last p on previous r, 2 ds, 2 ps sep by 2
ds, 2 ds, join to corresponding p on first motif,
2 ds, 3 ps sep by 2 ds, 3 ds, cl, rw. Ch of 3 ds, rw.
R of 3 ds, join to last p on previous lr, 3 ds, 2 ps
sep by 3 ds, 3 ds, cl, rw. Ch of 5 ds, join to p on
corresponding ch, 5 ds, rw. Sr of 4 ds, join to
last p on previous r, 4 ds, p, 4 ds, cl, rw. Ch of
9 ds, join to next p on previous row, 9 ds, rw;
repeat from * once more and complete as first
motif. Make 35 more motifs joining each as
second motif was joined to first, placing as
shown on diagram. Where 3 corners meet, join
3rd corner to joining of previous motifs.
Damp and pin out to measurements.

for colour illustration, see page 87
for diagram, see page 90

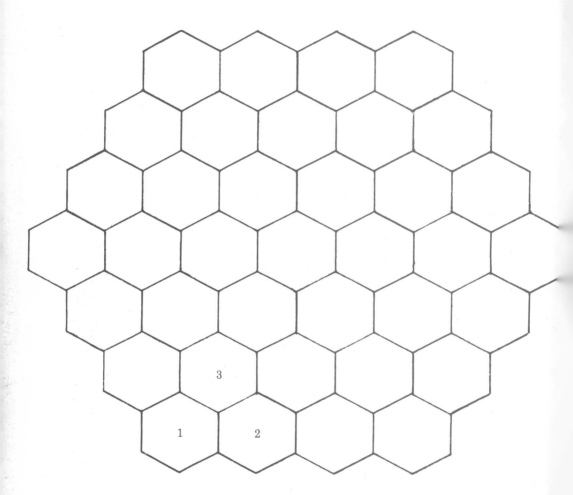

Traycloth with insertion

Materials: Coats Mercer–Crochet no. 40
(20 grms).
1 ball. This model is worked in Ecru.
Piece of Old Bleach linen, Biscuit, 15 × 21 ins.
Milward tatting shuttle.

Width of insertion: 1 in.

Measurements: 14½ × 20½ ins.

Mark 2 ins in from edge all round linen. Cut
out this rectangle 11 × 17 ins. (linen centre).
Turn back ¼ in for hems on inside and outside
edges of linen border. Trim linen centre to
measure 10 × 16 ins.
Turn back ¼ in for hems all round linen centre.
Slip stitch hems.

Insertion

1st row: Tie ball and shuttle threads together. R of 6 ds, 3 ps sep by 6 ds, 6 ds, cl, rw.
* Ch of 4 ds, 2 ps sep by 3 ds, 3 ds, rw. Sr of 3 ds,
join to last p of previous r, 3 ds, 2 ps sep by
3 ds, 3 ds, cl, * * rw. Ch of 3 ds, join to adjacent
p on previous ch, 3 ds, p, 4 ds, rw. R of 6 ds,
join to last p of previous sr, 6 ds, 2 ps sep by
6 ds, 6 ds, cl, rw; repeat from * for length
required to corner of linen centre, ending last
repeat at * *. Sr of 3 ds, join to last p of previous sr, 3 ds, 2 ps sep by 3 ds, 3 ds, cl; repeat
from first * * joining last p of last sr to first p
of first r and last ch to base of first r. Tie ends,
cut and oversew neatly on wrong side.

2nd row: Tie ball and shuttle threads together. R of 6 ds, p, 6 ds, join to p of first sr on
previous row, 6 ds, p, 6 ds, cl, rw. * Ch of 4 ds,
2 ps sep by 3 ds, 3 ds, rw. Sr of 3 ds, join to p of
previous r, 3 ds, join to p of next r on previous
row, 3 ds, p, 3 ds, cl, rw. Ch of 3 ds, join to
adjacent p on previous ch, 3 ds, p, 4 ds, * * rw.
R of 6 ds, join to p of previous sr, 6 ds, join to p
of next sr on previous row, 6 ds, p, 6 ds, cl, rw;
repeat from * to corner. Ch of 6 ds, 2 ps sep by
6 ds, 6 ds, rw. R of 6 ds, join to p of previous r,
6 ds, 2 ps sep by 6 ds, 6 ds, cl, rw. Ch as previous ch. R of 6 ds, join to p of previous r, 6 ds,
join to p of next sr on previous row, 6 ds, p, 6
ds, cl, rw; repeat from first * ending last repea
at * *, joining last p of last sr to first p of first
and last ch to base of first r. Tie ends, cut and
oversew neatly on wrong side.
Sew insertion neatly in place (see illustration
Damp and press.

for colour illustration, see page 91

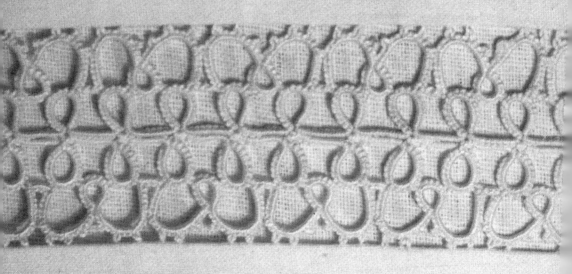

Pillowcase edging and insertion

Materials: Coats Mercer-Crochet no. 20
(20 grms).
2 balls. This model is worked in White.
1 pillowcase.
Milward tatting shuttle.

Width of insertion: $1\frac{7}{8}$ in.

Depth of edging: $\frac{7}{8}$ in.

Insertion

1st row: Tie ball and shuttle threads together. * R of 8 ds, 2 ps sep by 4 ds, 8 ds, cl. Ch
of 8 ds; repeat from * for length required, having an even number of chs between rs and
joining last ch to base of first r, without twist-
ing work, rw. * * R of 8 ds, 2 ps sep by 4 ds,
8 ds, cl. Ch of 8 ds, join by shuttle thread to
base of next r; repeat from * *, joining last ch
to base of first r. Tie ends, cut and oversew
neatly on wrong side.

2nd row: Tie ball and shuttle threads together. R of 5 ds, join to p at right of any r on
lower edge of previous row, 5 ds, join to next
p of next r, 5 ds, cl, rw. * Ch of 3 ds, 4 ps sep by
3 ds, 6 ds, join by shuttle thread to next p. Ch
of 3 ds, join by shuttle thread to next p. Ch of 6
ds, join to last p of adjacent ch, 3 ds, 3 ps sep
by 3 ds, 3 ds, rw. R of 5 ds, join to next p, 5 ds,
join to next p, 5 ds, cl, rw; repeat from * omitting r at end of last repeat and joining last ch
to base of first r. Tie ends, cut and oversew
neatly on wrong side.
Work other side to correspond.

Edging

1st row: Work as for first side of first row for
length required. Tie ends, cut and oversew
neatly on wrong side.

2nd row: Work as for first side of 2nd row. Tie
ends, cut and oversew neatly on wrong side.

To make up

Pin insertion in place $3\frac{1}{2}$ ins from edge of
pillowcase. Cut away surplus material at back
of insertion, leaving $\frac{1}{4}$ in for hem on each side.
Sew hems and insertion neatly in place,
attaching 2 ps of each ch, as in illustration.
Sew on edging, attaching at base of each r.
Damp and press.

for colour illustrations, see pages 94 and 95

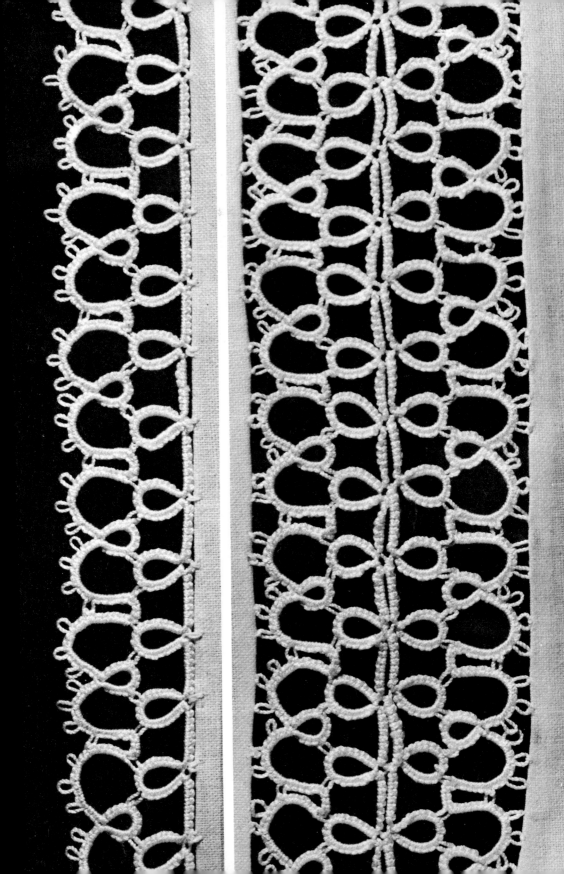

Long john runner

Materials: Coats Mercer-Crochet no. 20
(20 grms).
2 balls Cream and 3 balls Brown.
2 Milward tatting shuttles.

Size of motif: $2\frac{3}{4}$ ins square.

Measurement: $11 \times 35\frac{3}{4}$ ins.

First motif

1st row: Using shuttle with Cream, r of 5 ds,
5 ps sep by 2 ds, 5 ds, cl. (R of 5 ds, join to corresponding p of adjacent r, 2 ds, 4 ps sep by 2
ds, 5 ds, cl) twice. R of 5 ds, join to corresponding p of adjacent r, 2 ds, 3 ps sep by 2 ds, 2 ds,
join to corresponding p on first r, 5 ds, cl. Tie
ends, cut and oversew neatly on wrong side.

2nd row: Using shuttle with Brown and ball
of Cream, tie ball and shuttle threads together. R of 5 ds, join to first free p of any r, 5 ds
cl. Ch of 5 ds, rw. R of 5 ds, p, 5 ds, cl, rw. *
Ch of 6 ds, rw. R of 5 ds, p, 5 ds, rw (corner r
made). Ch of 6 ds, rw. R of 5 ds, p, 5 ds, cl, rw.
Ch of 5 ds. R of 5 ds, join to last free p on same
r of previous row, 5 ds, cl. Ch of 5 ds, rw. R of 5
ds, join to p of adjacent r, 5 ds, cl, rw. Ch of 4
ds, rw. R of 5 ds, p, 5 ds, cl, rw. Ch of 4 ds, rw.
R of 5 ds, p, 5 ds, cl, rw. Ch of 5 ds. * * R of 5 ds,
join to first free p on next r of previous row,
5 ds, cl. Ch of 5 ds, rw. R of 5 ds, join to p of
adjacent r, 5 ds, cl, rw; repeat from * 3 times
more ending last repeat at * *, joining last r to
second r correspond and joining last ch to
base of first r. Tie ends, cut and oversew
neatly on wrong side.

for detail, see page 101

3rd row: Using shuttle with Brown and ball of Cream, tie ball and shuttle threads together. R of 5 ds, join to any corner p, 5 ds, cl, rw. * Ch of 3 ds, p, 3 ds, rw. R of 5 ds, join to same p as last r, 5 ds, cl, rw. Ch of 3 ds, 3 ps sep by 3 ds, 3 ds, rw. R of 5 ds, join to same p as last r, 5 ds, cl, rw. Ch of 3 ds, p, 3 ds, rw. R of 5 ds, join to same p as last r, 5 ds, cl, rw. Ch of 3 ds, p, 3 ds, join by shuttle thread to p at joining of next 2 rs. Ch of 3 ds, p, 3 ds, rw. R of 5 ds, join to p of next r, 5 ds, cl, rw. Ch of 3 ds, 3 ps sep by 3 ds, 3 ds, rw. R of 5 ds, join to same p as last r, 5 ds, cl, rw. Ch of 3 ds, p, 3 ds, join by shuttle thread to p at joining of next 2 rs. Ch of 3 ds, p, 3 ds, rw. * * R of 5 ds, join to next corner p. 5 ds, cl, rw; repeat from * 3 times more, ending last repeat at * * joining last ch to base of first r. Tie ends, cut and oversew neatly on wrong side.

Second motif

Work as first motif for 2 rows.

3rd row: Using shuttle with Brown and ball of Cream, tie ball and shuttle threads together. R of 5 ds, join to any corner p, 5 ds, cl, rw. Ch of 3 ds, p, 3 ds, rw. R of 5 ds, join to same p as last r, 5 ds, cl, rw. Ch of 3 ds, 2 ps sep by 3 ds, 3 ds, join to corresponding p on first motif, 3 ds, rw. R of 5 ds, join to same p as last r, 5 ds, cl, rw. Ch of 3 ds, p, 3 ds, rw. R of 5 ds, join to same p as last r, 5 ds, cl, rw. Ch of 3 ds, p, 3 ds, join by shuttle thread to p at joining of next 2 rs. Ch of 3 ds, p, 3 ds, rw. R of 5 ds, join to p of next r, 5 ds, cl, rw. Ch of 3 ds, p 3 ds, join to corresponding p on first motif, 3 ds, p, 3 ds, rw. R of 5 ds, join to same p as last r, 5 ds, cl, rw. Ch of 3 ds, p, 3 ds, join by shuttle thread to p at joining of next 2 rs. Ch of 3 ds, p, 3 ds, rw. R of 5 ds, join to next corner p, 5 ds, cl, rw. Ch of 3 ds, p, 3 ds, rw. R of 5 ds, join to same p as last r, 5 ds, cl, rw. Ch of 3 ds, join to corresponding p on first motif, 3 ds, 2 ps sep by 3 ds, 3 ds, rw and complete as first motif.
Make 4 rows of 13 motifs, joining adjacent sides as second motif was joined to first motif. Damp and pin out to measurements.

Motif cheval set

Materials: Coats Mercer-Crochet no. 20
(20 grms).
4 balls. This model is worked in Amber Gold.
Milward tatting shuttle.

Size of motif: 2 ins from point to point.

Measurements:
Centrepiece – 20 × 10 ins.
Small mat – 6 ins square.

Centrepiece
First motif

1st row: R of 2 ds, 8 ps sep by 3 ds, 1 ds, cl. Tie
ends, cut and oversew neatly on wrong side.

2nd row: Tie ball and shuttle threads
together. Attach thread to any p on previous
row. Ch of 8 ds. (R of 6 ds, p, 6 ds, cl) 3 times.
* Ch of 8 ds, join by shuttle thread to same p
on previous row. Ch of 3 ds, join by shuttle
thread to next p on previous row. * * Ch of 8
ds. R of 6 ds, join to p of last r, 6 ds, cl. (R of 6
ds, p, 6 ds, cl) twice; repeat from * ending last
repeat at * *, joining last r to first r and last ch
to same place as first ch. Tie ends, cut and
oversew neatly on wrong side.

for detail, see page 102
for colour illustration, see page 103

Second motif

Work as first motif for 1 row.

2nd row: Tie ball and shuttle threads
together. Attach thread to any p on previous
row. Ch of 8 ds. R of 6 ds, p, 6 ds, cl. * R of 6 ds,
join to corresponding p on first motif, 6 ds, cl.
R of 6 ds, p, 6 ds, cl. Ch of 8 ds, join by shuttle
thread to same p on previous row. Ch of 3 ds,
join by shuttle thread to next p on previous
row. Ch of 8 ds. R of 6 ds, join to p of last r, 6
ds, cl; repeat from * once more and complete
as first motif.
Make 10 rows of 5 motifs, joining adjacent
sides as second motif was joined to first.

Filling

1st row: R of 1 ds, 8 ps sep by 2 ds, 1 ds, cl. Tie
ends, cut and oversew neatly on wrong side.

2nd row: Tie ball and shuttle threads
together. Attach thread to any p on previous
row. Ch of 8 ds, join to p at joining of any 2
motifs, 8 ds, join by shuttle thread to same p
on previous row. * Ch of 2 ds, join by shuttle
thread to next p on previous row. Ch of 8 ds,
join to p at joining of next 2 rs, 8 ds, join by
shuttle thread to same p on previous row. Ch
of 2 ds, join by shuttle thread to next p on previous row. * * Ch of 8 ds, join to p at joining of
next 2 motifs, 8 ds, join by shuttle thread to
same p on previous row; repeat from * ending
last repeat at * * and joining last ch to same
place as first ch. Tie ends, cut and oversew
neatly on wrong side.

Small mat *make 2*

Make 3 rows of 3 motifs joining as before, having 4 filling motifs.
Damp and pin out to measurements.

Motif luncheon set

Materials: Coats Mercer-Crochet no. 10
(20 grms).
8 balls. This model is worked in Lt French
Blue.
The above quantity is sufficient for one centrepiece and one place mat.
Milward tatting shuttle.

Size of motif: 1¾ in diameter.

Measurements:
Centrepiece – 14¾ × 19½ ins approximately.
Place mat – 14¾ × 16½ ins approximately.

Centrepiece

First motif
R of 10 ds, 3 ps sep by 4 ds, 10 ds, cl. * R of 10
ds, join to last p of previous r, 4 ds, 2 ps sep by
4 ds, 10 ds, cl; repeat from * 10 times more,
joining last p of last r to first p of first r. Tie
ends, cut and oversew neatly on wrong side.

Second motif
R of 10 ds, p, 4 ds, join to centre p of any r on
first motif, 4 ds, p, 10 ds, cl. R of 10 ds, join to
last p of previous r, 4 ds, join to p of next r on
first motif, 4 ds, p, 10 ds, cl.
Complete as for first motif.
Work 7 rows of 10 motifs, joining adjacent
sides as second motif was joined to first motif
leaving one free p between joins.

for colour illustration, see page 107

Border

1st row: Tie ball and shuttle threads together. Attach thread to free p to right of centre free p on any corner. * Ch of 3 ds, 2 ps sep by 3 ds, 3 ds, join by shuttle thread to next p. Ch of 4 ds, 5 ps sep by 4 ds, 4 ds, join by shuttle thread to 2nd free p on next motif; repeat from * to next corner motif. Ch of 3 ds, 2 ps sep by 3 ds, 3 ds, join by shuttle thread to next p. Ch of 4 ds, 5 ps sep by 4 ds, 4 ds, miss 1 p, join by shuttle thread to next p; repeat from first * joining last ch to same place as first ch. Tie ends, cut and oversew neatly on wrong side.

2nd row: Tie ball and shuttle threads together. Work 5 rs as for first motif. Ch of 3 ds, 2 ps sep by 3 ds, 4 ds, join by shuttle thread to 5th p of second ch on previous row. * Ch of 4 ds, 2 ps sep by 3 ds, 3 ds, join to last p of previous r, 3 ds, 4 ps sep by 3 ds, 4 ds, miss 2 ps on previous row, join by shuttle thread to next p. Ch of 4 ds, 2 ps sep by 3 ds, 3 ds. * * R of 10 ds, join to 3rd p of 2nd last ch, 4 ds, 2 ps sep by 4 ds, 10 ds, cl. Work 4 rs as for first motif. Ch of 3 ds, 2 ps sep by 3 ds, 4 ds, miss 3 ps on previous row, join by shuttle thread to next p; repeat from * to next corner but only miss 1 p on corner ch at end of last repeat. Ch of 4 ds, 2 ps sep by 3 ds, 3 ds. R of 10 ds, join to last p of previous r, 4 ds, 2 ps sep by 4 ds, 10 ds, cl. Work 4 rs as for first motif. Ch of 3 ds, 2 ps sep by 3 ds, 4 ds, miss 1 p on previous row, join by shuttle thread to next p; repeat from first * ending last repeat at * * joining second last ch to first p of first r and last ch to base of same r. Tie ends, cut and oversew neatly on wrong side.

Place mat

Work 7 rows of 8 motifs joining as before.
Work border as for centrepiece.
Damp and press.

Coffee table mat

Materials: Coats Mercer-Crochet no. 10
(20 grms).
3 balls. This model is worked in Ecru.
Milward tatting shuttle.

Tension (gauge): First row 1⅞ in diameter.

Measurement: 19 ins diameter, approximately.

1st row: Tie ball and shuttle threads together. R of 3 ds, 5 ps sep by 3 ds, 3 ds, cl, rw.
* Ch of 3 ds, 3 ps sep by 3 ds, 3 ds, rw. R of 3 ds,
p, 3 ds, join to 2nd last p on previous r, 3 ds,
3 ps sep by 3 ds, 3 ds, cl, rw; repeat from * 8
times more joining 2nd last p of last r to 2nd p
on first r. Ch of 3 ds, 3 ps sep by 3 ds, 3 ds, join
to base of first r. Tie ends, cut and oversew
neatly on wrong side.

for colour illustration, see page 111

2nd row: Tie ball and shuttle threads together. Attach thread to centre p of any ch on
previous row. Ch of 4 ds, p, * 6 ds, 2 ps sep by
4 ds, 6 ds, * * p, 4 ds, join by shuttle thread to
centre p of next ch on previous row, 4 ds, join
to last p on adjacent ch; repeat from * ending
last repeat at * *, join to first p on first ch,
4 ds, join to same p as first ch was attached.
Tie ends, cut and oversew neatly on wrong
side.

3rd row: Tie ball and shuttle threads together. R of 3 ds, 5 ps sep by 3 ds, 3 ds, cl, rw.
Ch of 6 ds, join to first free p of ch on previous
row, 3 ds, p, 6 ds. [R of 3 ds, 5 ps sep by 3 ds,
3 ds, cl, rw. Ch of 4 ds, join to 2nd last p on
adjacent r, 3 ds, 2 ps sep by 3 ds, 4 ds, rw. * (R
of 3 ds, p, 3 ds, join to 2nd last p on previous r,
3 ds, 3 ps sep by 3 ds, 3 ds, cl, rw]. Ch of 4 ds,
3 ps sep by 3 ds, 4 ds, rw) 7 times. R of 3 ds, p,
3 ds, join to 2nd last p on previous r, 3 ds, p,
3 ds, join to 2nd p on adjacent r, 3 ds, p, 3 ds, cl.
Ch of 6 ds, join to p on adjacent ch, 3 ds, join to
next p of ch on previous row, 6 ds, rw. R of 3
ds, p, 3 ds, join to first p on adjacent ch, 3 ds,
3 ps sep by 3 ds, 3 ds, cl, rw. Ch of 6 ds, join to
first p of next ch on previous row, 3 ds, p, 6 ds.
Repeat within [ ] once. Ch of 4 ds, p, 3 ds, join
to corresponding p on adjacent ch, 3 ds, p, 4 ds,
rw; * * repeat from * working within ( ) 6 times
and ending last repeat at * *. Repeat within
( ) 4 times. R as before, rw. Ch of 4 ds, p, 3 ds,
join to corresponding p on adjacent ch, 3 ds, p,
4 ds, rw. R as before, rw. Ch of 6 ds, 2 ps sep by
3 ds, 3 ds, join to 2nd p of first r, 4 ds, rw. R of 3
ds, p, 3 ds, join to 2nd p on previous r, 3 ds, p,
3 ds, join to 2nd p on adjacent r, 3 ds, p, 3 ds, cl.
rw. Ch of 6 ds, join to p on adjacent ch, 3 ds,
join to next p on previous row, 6 ds, join to
base of first r. Tie ends, cut and oversew
neatly on wrong side.

4th row: Tie ball and shuttle threads together. R of 2 ds, 3 ps sep by 3 ds, 3 ds, join to centre p of 6th 3 p ch on previous row, 4 ds, p, 4 ds, join to centre p on adjacent ch, 3 ds, 3 ps sep by 3 ds, 2 ds, cl, rw. * Ch of 4 ds, 6 ps sep by 2 ds, 4 ds, join by shuttle thread to centre p on next ch, 4 ds, 5 ps sep by 2 ds, 4 ds, join by shuttle thread to centre p on next ch, 4 ds, 6 ps sep by 2 ds, 4 ds, * * rw. R of 2 ds, 3 ps sep by 3 ds, 3 ds, join to centre p on next ch, 4 ds, p, 4 ds, join to centre p on next ch, 3 ds, 3 ps sep by 3 ds, 2 ds, cl, rw; repeat from * ending last repeat at * *, join to base of first r. Tie ends, cut and oversew neatly on wrong side.

5th row: Tie ball and shuttle threads together. R of 8 ds, join to last p of last ch on previous row, 3 ds, join to first p on next ch, 8 ds, cl, rw. Ch of 4 ds, p, * 7 ds, p, 9 ds, p, 4 ds, miss 2 ps on previous row, join by shuttle thread to next p, 4 ds, join to corresponding p on adjacent ch, 9 ds, p, 7 ds, p, 4 ds, rw. R of 8 ds, miss 4 ps on previous row, join to next p, 8 ds, cl, rw. Ch of 4 ds, join to corresponding p on adjacent ch, 7 ds, p, 9 ds, p, 4 ds, miss 4 ps on previous row, join by shuttle thread to next p, 4 ds, join to corresponding p on adjacent ch, 9 ds, p, 7 ds, * * p, 4 ds, rw. R of 8 ds, miss 2 ps, join to next p, 3 ds, join to next p, 8 ds, cl, rw. Ch of 4 ds, join to corresponding p on adjacent ch; repeat from * ending last repeat at * *, join to first p on first ch, 4 ds, join to base of first r. Tie ends, cut and oversew neatly on wrong side.

6th row: Tie ball and shuttle threads together. R of 2 ds, 7 ps sep by 3 ds, 2 ds, cl, rw. Ch of 6 ds, p, 3 ds, join to free p of first ch on previous row, 3 ds, p, 6 ds. * R of 3 ds, 5 ps sep by 3 ds, 3 ds, cl, rw. Ch of 4 ds, 2 ps sep by 3 ds, 3 ds, join to 3rd p of adjacent r, 4 ds, rw. (R of

3 ds, p, 3 ds, join to 2nd last p of last r, 3 ds, 3 ps sep by 3 ds, 3 ds, cl, rw. * Ch of 4 ds, 3 ps sep by 3 ds, 4 ds, rw) 7 times. * * R of 3 ds, p, 3 ds, join to 2nd last p of previous r, 3 ds, p, 3 ds, join to 2nd p of adjacent r, 3 ds, p, 3 ds, cl. Ch of 6 ds, p, 3 ds, join to p of next ch on previous row, 3 ds, p, 6 ds, rw. R of 2 ds, 2 ps sep by 3 ds, 3 ds, join to 3rd p on adjacent ch, 3 ds, 4 ps sep by 3 ds, 2 ds, cl, rw. Ch of 6 ds, p, 3 ds, join to p of next ch on previous row, 3 ds, p, 6 ds. Repeat from * to * once. Ch of 4 ds, p, 3 ds, join to corresponding p of adjacent ch, 3 ds, p, 4 ds, rw. * * * Repeat within ( ) 6 times; repeat from * * ending last repeat at * * *. Repeat within ( ) 4 times. R as before, rw. Ch of 4 ds, p, 3 ds, join to corresponding p of adjacent ch, 3 ds, p, 4 ds, rw. R as before, rw. Ch of 4 ds, join to 2nd p of adjacent r, 3 ds, 2 ps sep by 3 ds, 4 ds, rw. R of 3 ds, p, 3 ds, join to 2nd last p of previous r, 3 ds, p, 3 ds, join to 2nd p of adjacent r, 3 ds, cl. Ch of 6 ds, p, 3 ds, join to p of next ch on previous row, 3 ds, p, 6 ds, join to base of first r. Tie ends, cut and oversew neatly on wrong side.

7th row: As 4th row.

8th row: Tie ball and shuttle threads together. R of 8 ds, miss 2 ps on first ch on previous row, join to next p, 2 ds, join to next p, 8 ds, cl, rw. * Ch of (10 ds, p) twice, 4 ds, miss 4 ps on previous row, join by shuttle thread to next p, 4 ds, join to corresponding p on adjacent ch, (10 ds, p, 10 ds, rw. R of 8 ds, miss 4 ps on previous row, join to next p, 2 ds, join to next p, 8 ds, cl, rw) twice; repeat from * omitting r at end of last repeat, join to base of first r. Tie ends, cut and oversew neatly on wrong side.

9th row: As 6th row.
Damp and pin out to measurements.

Cheval set

Materials: Coats Mercer-Crochet no. 20
(20 grms).
2 balls. This model is worked in Blush Pink.
Milward tatting shuttle.

Measurements:
Centrepiece – 16 × 10½ ins approximately.
Small mat – 6¾ ins from point to point.

Centrepiece

Tie ball and shuttle threads together.

1st row: *1st ring* – R of 12 ds, p, 12 ds, cl. *2nd
ring* – R of 10 ds, 2 ps sep by 3 ds, 10 ds, cl, rw.
1st p chain – Ch of 5 ds, p, 8 ds, 2 ps sep by 8 ds,
8 ds, rw. *3rd ring* – R of 12 ds, join to base of
last r, 12 ds, cl. Repeat 2nd ring. *2nd p chain* –
Ch of 8 ds, join to corresponding p on adjacent
ch, 8 ds, 2 ps sep by 8 ds, 5 ds, p, 5 ds, rw.
Repeat 3rd and 2nd rings once more, rw. *3rd p
chain* – (Ch of 5 ds, join to corresponding p on
adjacent ch) twice, 8 ds, 2 ps sep by 8 ds, 5 ds,
p, 5 ds, rw. Repeat 3rd ring, rw. * Ch of 5 ds,
rw. Repeat 2nd ring, rw. Ch of 5 ds, join to
base of adjacent r. Repeat 3rd p chain, rw. *9th
ring* – R of 12 ds, join to base of same r as ch
was joined, 12 ds, cl, * rw. Ch of 8 ds, rw.
Repeat 2nd ring, rw. Ch of 8 ds, join to base of
adjacent r. Repeat 3rd p chain, rw. Repeat 9th
ring, rw. Repeat from * to * once more. Repeat
2nd ring, rw. (Ch of 5 ds, join to corresponding
p on adjacent ch) twice, 8 ds, 2 ps sep by 8 ds,
8 ds, rw. Repeat 3rd and 2nd rings, rw. Ch of
8 ds, join to corresponding p on adjacent ch,
8 ds, 2 ps sep by 8 ds, 5 ds, rw. Repeat 3rd and
2nd rings, rw. Ch of 5 ds, join to corresponding
p on adjacent ch, 8 ds, p, 8 ds, rw. Repeat 3rd
ring. Sr of 4 ds, 2 ps sep by 3 ds, 4 ds, cl, rw. Ch
of 8 ds, rw. R of 12 ds, 2 ps sep by 3 ds, 12 ds, cl,
rw. Ch of 8 ds, rw. Sr as before, rw. Ch of 8 ds,
join to p on corresponding ch, 8 ds, p, 5 ds, rw.
R of 12 ds, join to base of last sr, 12 ds, cl.
Repeat 2nd ring, rw. *11th p chain* – Ch of 5 ds,
join to corresponding p on adjacent ch, 8 ds,
join to free p on corresponding ch, 8 ds, p, 8 ds,
rw. Repeat 3rd and 2nd rings, rw. *12th p chain*
– Ch of 8 ds, join to corresponding p on adjacent ch, 8 ds, join to p on corresponding ch, 8
ds, 2 ps sep by 5 ds, 5 ds, rw. Repeat 3rd and
2nd rings, rw. *13th p chain* – (Ch of 5 ds, join to

for colour illustration, see page 115
for detail, see page 117

112

corresponding p on adjacent ch) twice, 8 ds, join to p on corresponding ch, 8 ds, 2 ps sep by 5 ds, 5 ds, rw. Repeat 3rd ring, rw. * * Ch of 5 ds, rw. Repeat 2nd ring, rw. Ch of 5 ds, join to base of adjacent r. Repeat 13th p chain, rw. Repeat 9th ring, * * rw. Ch of 8 ds, rw. Repeat 2nd ring rw. Ch of 8 ds, join to base of adjacent r. Repeat 13th p chain, rw. Repeat 9th ring, rw. Repeat from * * to * * once more. Repeat 2nd ring, rw. (Ch of 5 ds, join to corresponding p on adjacent ch) twice, 8 ds, join to p on corresponding ch, 8 ds, p, 8 ds, rw. Repeat 3rd and 2nd rings, rw. Ch of 8 ds, join to p on adjacent ch, 8 ds, join to p on corresponding ch, 8 ds, p, 5 ds, rw. Repeat 3rd and 2nd rings, rw. Ch of 5 ds, join to p on adjacent ch, 8 ds, p, 8 ds, rw. Repeat 3rd ring. Sr of 4 ds, 2 ps sep by 3 ds, 4 ds, cl, rw. Ch of 8 ds, rw. R of 12 ds, 2 ps sep by 3 ds, 12 ds, cl, rw. Ch of 8 ds, rw. Sr of 4 ds, 2 ps sep by 3 ds, 4 ds, join to p on first r worked, cl, rw. Ch of 8 ds, join to p on corresponding ch, 8 ds, join to adjacent p on first ch worked, 5 ds, join to base of first r. Tie ends, cut and oversew neatly on wrong side.

2nd row: Tie ball and shuttle threads together. R of 12 ds, join to first free p on 2nd last sr, 3 ds, join to next p, 8 ds, p, 12 ds, cl, rw. Ch of 12 ds, 2 ps sep by 12 ds, 12 ds, join by shuttle thread to p on last r, rw. * R of 12 ds, join to first p of next r on previous row, 3 ds, p, 12 ds, cl, rw. Chain as before, rw. (R of 3 ds, join to next p on previous row, 12 ds, join to first p of next r on previous row, 3 ds, p, 15 ds, cl, rw. Chain as before, rw) 8 times. R of 3 ds, join to next p on previous row, 12 ds, p, 15 ds, cl, rw. Chain as before, rw. R of 12 ds, join to first p of next sr, 3 ds, join to next p, 8 ds, p, 12 ds, cl, rw. Chain as before, rw. R of 8 ds, join to first p of next r on previous row, 8 ds, p, 12 ds, cl, rw. Chain as before, rw. * * R of 8 ds, join to

p of r on previous row, 8 ds, p, 12 ds, cl, rw. Chain as before, rw. R of 12 ds, join to first p on next sr, 3 ds, join to next p, 8 ds, p, 12 ds, cl, rw. Chain as before, rw; repeat from * to * * once more. R of 8 ds, join to next p on previous row, 8 ds, join to base of first r, 12 ds, cl, rw. Chain as before, join to base of first r. Tie ends, cut and oversew neatly on wrong side.

3rd row: Tie ball and shuttle threads together. R of 3 ds, 4 ps sep by 3 ds, 3 ds, join to first p of last ch on previous row, 3 ds, 3 ps sep by 3 ds, 3 ds, cl, rw. * Ch of 4 ds, 5 ps sep by 2 ds, 4 ds, rw. R of 3 ds, 3 ps sep by 3 ds, 3 ds, join to next p of same ch on previous row, 3 ds, join to first p of next ch on previous row, 3 ds, 3 ps sep by 3 ds, 3 ds, cl, rw; repeat from * 12 times more. Chain as before, rw. R of 3 ds, 3 ps sep by 3 ds, 3 ds, join to next p of same ch on previous row, 3 ds, 4 ps sep by 3 ds, 3 ds, cl, rw. Chain as before, rw. R of 3 ds, 2 ps sep by 3 ds, 3 ds, join to corresponding p on last r, 3 ds, 5 ps sep by 3 ds, 3 ds, cl, rw. Ch of 4 ds, 8 ps sep by 2 ds, 4 ds, rw. * * R of 3 ds, 2 ps sep by 3 ds, 3 ds, join to corresponding p on last r, 3 ds, 5 ps sep by 3 ds, cl, rw. Ch of 4 ds, 5 ps sep by 2 ds, 4 ds, rw. R of 3 ds, 2 ps sep by 3 ds, 3 ds, join to corresponding p on last r, 3 ds, p, 3 ds, join to first p of next ch on previous row, 3 ds, 3 ps sep by 3 ds, 3 ds, cl, rw; repeat from first * to * * once more. R of 3 ds, 2 ps sep by 3 ds, join to corresponding p on last r, 3 ds, 2 ps sep by 3 ds, 3 ds, join to corresponding p on first r, 3 ds, 2 ps sep by 3 ds, 3 ds, cl rw. Ch of 4 ds, 5 ps sep by 2 ds, 4 ds, join to base of first r. Tie ends, cut and oversew neatly on wrong side.

4th row: Tie ball and shuttle threads together. R of 2 ds, 3 ps sep by 2 ds, 2 ds, join to last p of last ch on previous row, 3 ds, join to first p on next ch, 2 ds, 3 ps sep by 2 ds, 2 ds, cl, rw. * Ch of 3 ds, 7 ps sep by 2 ds, 3 ds, p, 8 ds, miss 3 ps on previous row, join by shuttle thread to next p, 2 ds, join by shuttle thread to first p on next ch, 8 ds, join to corresponding p on adjacent ch, * * 3 ds, 7 ps sep by 2 ds, 3 ds, rw. R of 2 ds, 3 ps sep by 2 ds, 2 ds, miss 3 ps on previous row, join to next p, 3 ds, join to first p on next ch, 2 ds, 3 ps sep by 2 ds, 2 ds, cl, rw; * * * repeat from * 6 times more and from * to * * once. Ch of 3 ds, 8 ps sep by 2 ds, 3 ds, rw. R of 2 ds, 3 ps sep by 2 ds, 2 ds, miss 2 ps in previous row, join to next p, 3 ds, join to next p, 2 ds, 3 ps sep by 2 ds, 2 ds, cl, rw. Ch of 3 ds, 8 ps sep by 2 ds, 3 ds, p, 8 ds, miss 2 ps on previous row, join by shuttle thread to next p, 2 ds, join by shuttle thread to first p on next ch, 8 ds, join to corrsponding p on adjacent ch, 3 ds, 7 ps sep by 2 ds, 3 ds, rw. R of 2 ds, 3 ps sep by 2 ds, 2 ds, miss 3 ps on previous row, join to next p, 3 ds, join to first p on next ch, 2 ds, 3 ps sep by 2 ds, 2 ds, cl, rw. Repeat from * to * * * 7 times and from * to * * once. Ch of 3 ds, 8 ps sep by 2 ds, 3 ds, rw. R of 2 ds, 3 ps sep by 2 ds, 2 ds, miss 2 ps on previous row, join to next p, 3 ds, join to next p, 2 ds, 3 ps sep by 2 ds, 2 ds, cl, rw. Ch of 3 ds, 8 ps sep by 2 ds, 3 ds, p, 8 ds, miss 2 ps on previous row, join by shuttle thread to next p, 2 ds, join by shuttle thread to first p on next ch, 8 ds, join to corresponding p on adjacent ch, 3 ds, 7 ps sep by 2 ds, 3 ds, join to base of first r. Tie ends, cut and oversew neatly on wrong side.

5th row: Tie ball and shuttle threads together. R of 2 ds, 3 ps sep by 2 ds, 2 ds, join to last free p of 2nd last ch on previous row, 3 ds, join to first p on next ch, 2 ds, 3 ps sep by 2 ds, 2 ds, cl, rw. * Ch of 3 ds, 7 ps sep by 2 ds, 3 ds, p, 8 ds, miss 5 ps on previous row, join by shuttle thread to next p, 2 ds, join by shuttle thread to first p on next ch, 8 ds, join to corres-

ponding p on adjacent ch, 3 ds, 7 ps sep by 2 ds, 3 ds, rw. R of 2 ds, 3 ps sep by 2 ds, 2 ds, miss 5 ps on previous row, join to next p, 3 ds, join to first p on next ch, 2 ds, 3 ps sep by 2 ds, 2 ds, cl, rw; * * repeat from * 7 times more. Ch of 3 ds, 10 ps sep by 2 ds, 3 ds, p, 8 ds, miss 6 ps on previous row, join by shuttle thread to next p, 2 ds, join by shuttle thread to first p on next ch, 8 ds, join to corresponding p on adjacent ch, 3 ds, 10 ps sep by 2 ds, 3 ds, rw. R of 2 ds, 3 ps sep by 2 ds, 2 ds, miss 6 ps on previous row, join to next p, 3 ds, join to first p on next ch, 2 ds, 3 ps sep by 2 ds, 2 ds, cl, rw; repeat from * to * * 8 times. Ch of 3 ds, 10 ps sep by 2 ds, 3 ds, p, 8 ds, miss 6 ps on previous row, join by shuttle thread to next p, 2 ds, join to first p on next ch, 8 ds, join to corresponding p on adjacent ch, 3 ds, 10 ps sep by 2 ds, 3 ds, join to base of first r. Tie ends, cut and oversew neatly on wrong side.

6th row: Tie ball and shuttle threads together. R of 2 ds, 3 ps sep by 2 ds, 2 ds, join to last free p of first ch on previous row, 3 ds, join to first p on next ch, 2 ds, 3 ps sep by 2 ds, 2 ds, cl, rw. * Ch of 3 ds, 8 ps sep by 2 ds, 3 ds, p, 8 ds, miss 5 ps on previous row, join by shuttle thread to next p, 2 ds, join by shuttle thread to first p on next ch, 8 ds, join to corresponding p on adjacent ch, 3 ds, 8 ps sep by 2 ds, 3 ds, rw. * * R of 2 ds, 3 ps sep by 2 ds, 2 ds, miss 5 ps on previous row, join to next p, 3 ds, join to first p on next ch, 2 ds, 3 ps sep by 2 ds, 2 ds, cl, rw; * * * repeat from * 6 times more and from * to * * once. R of 2 ds, 3 ps sep by 2 ds, 2 ds, miss 5 ps on previous row, join to next p, 3 ds, 4 ps sep by 2 ds, 2 ds, cl, rw. Ch of 3 ds, 10 ps sep by 2 ds, 3 ds, rw. R of 2 ds, 3 ps sep by 2 ds, 2 ds, join to corresponding p on last r, 3 ds, miss 3 ps on next ch, join to next p, 2 ds, 3 ps sep by 2 ds, cl, rw; repeat from first * to * * * 8

times and from * to * * once. R of 2 ds, 3 ps sep by 2 ds, 2 ds, miss 5 ps on previous row, join to next p, 3 ds, 4 ps sep by 2 ds, 2 ds, cl, rw. Ch of 3 ds, 10 ps sep by 2 ds, 3 ds, rw. R of 2 ds, 3 ps sep by 2 ds, join to corresponding p on previous r, 3 ds, miss 3 ps on next ch, join to next p, 2 ds, 3 ps sep by 2 ds, 2 ds, cl, rw; repeat from * to * * joining last ch to base of first r. Tie ends, cut and oversew neatly on wrong side.

7th row: Tie ball and shuttle threads together. R of 3 ds, p, 3 ds, join to last p of last ch on previous row, 3 ds, join to first p on next ch, 3 ds, 3 ps sep by 3 ds, 3 ds, cl, rw. (Ch of 3 ds, 4 ps sep by 3 ds, 3 ds, rw. R of 3 ds, p, 3 ds, join to corresponding p on last r, 3 ds, 4 ps sep by 3 ds, 3 ds, cl, rw) 5 times. [Ch of 3 ds, 4 ps sep by 3 ds, 3 ds, rw. R of 3 ds, p, 3 ds, join to corresponding p on last r, 3 ds, p, 3 ds, join to last p of next ch on previous row, 3 ds, join to first p on next ch, 3 ds, p, 3 ds, cl, rw. Ch of 3 ds, join to corresponding p on adjacent ch, 3 ds, 3 ps sep by 3 ds, 3 ds, rw. R of 3 ds, p, 3 ds, miss 6 ps on previous row, join to next p, 3 ds, join to first p on next ch, 3 ds, 3 ps sep by 3 ds, 3 ds, cl, rw]. * Ch of 3 ds, join to corresponding p on adjacent ch, 3 ds, 3 ps sep by 3 ds, 3 ds, rw. R of 3 ds, p, 3 ds, join to corresponding p on last r, 3 ds, 4 ps sep by 3 ds, 3 ds, cl, rw. * * * (Ch of 3 ds, 4 ps sep by 3 ds, 3 ds, rw. R of 3 ds, p, 3 ds, join to corresponding p on last r, 3 ds, 4 ps sep by 3 ds, 3 ds, cl, rw) 4 times. * * Repeat within [ ] once more. * * * Repeat from * 4 times more ending at * * at end of last repeat. * * * * Ch of 3 ds, 4 ps sep by 3 ds, 3 ds, join by shuttle thread to second p on last r, rw. Lr of 3 ds, join to next p on last r, 3 ds, 3 ps sep by 3 ds, 3 ds, join to 5th p of corner ch on previous row, 3 ds, join to next p, 3 ds, 4 ps sep by 3 ds, 3 ds, cl, rw. Ch of 3 ds, join to corresponding p on adjacent ch, 3 ds, 3 ps sep by 3 ds, 3 ds, rw.

R of 3 ds, p, 3 ds, join to base of lr, 3 ds, join to last p on lr, 3 ds, 3 ps sep by 3 ds, 3 ds, cl, rw. * * * * Repeat from * * * to * * * once more then from first * to second * * * 6 times more ending last repeat at * *. Repeat from * * * * to * * * * once more. Repeat from * * * to * * * once more omitting last r at end of last repeat and joining last p of last ch to first p of first ch, join to base of first r. Tie ends, cut and oversew neatly on wrong side.

Small mat *make 2*

1st row: Tie ball and shuttle threads together. R of 14 ds, p, 12 ds, cl, rw. * Ch of 12 ds, 2 ps sep by 12 ds, 12 ds, join by shuttle thread to p on last r, rw. * * R of 14 ds, p, 12 ds, cl, rw; repeat from * 4 times more and from * to * * once joining last ch to base of first r. Tie ends, cut and oversew neatly on wrong side.

2nd row: Tie ball and shuttle threads together. R of 3 ds, 3 ps sep by 3 ds, 3 ds, join to first p of first ch on previous row, 3 ds, 4 ps sep by 3 ds, 3 ds, cl, rw. * Ch of 4 ds, 6 ps sep by 2 ds, 4 ds, rw. R of 3 ds, 2 ps sep by 3 ds, 3 ds, join to corresponding p on last r, 3 ds, p, 3 ds, join to next p on previous row, 3 ds, 3 ps sep by 3 ds, 3 ds, cl, rw. Ch as before. R of 3 ds, 2 ps sep by 3 ds, 3 ds, join to corresponding p on last r, 3 ds, 5 ps sep by 3 ds, 3 ds, cl, rw. Ch as before. * * R of 3 ds, 2 ps sep by 3 ds, 3 ds, join to corresponding p on last r, 3 ds, join to first p of next ch on previous row, 3 ds, 4 ps sep by 3 ds, 3 ds, cl, rw; repeat from * ending last repeat at * * joining corresponding p of last r to 3rd p of first r. Tie ends, cut and oversew neatly on wrong side.

3rd row: Tie ball and shuttle threads together. R of 2 ds, 3 ps sep by 2 ds, 2 ds, join to last p of last ch on previous row, 4 ds, join to first p on next ch, 2 ds, 3 ps sep by 2 ds, 2 ds, cl, rw. * Ch of 3 ds, 8 ps sep by 3 ds, 8 ds, miss 4 ps on previous row, join by shuttle thread to next p, 2 ds, join by shuttle thread to first p on next ch, 8 ds, join to corresponding p on adjacent ch, 3 ds, 7 ps sep by 3 ds, 3 ds, * * rw. R of 2 ds, 3 ps sep by 2 ds, 2 ds, miss 4 ps on previous row, join to next p, 4 ds, join to first p on next ch, 2 ds, 3 ps sep by 2 ds, 2 ds, cl, rw; repeat from * ending last repeat at * * and joining last ch to base of first r. Tie ends, cut and oversew neatly on wrong side.

4th row: Tie ball and shuttle threads together. R of 2 ds, p, 3 ds, join to last p before any r on previous row, 3 ds, join to first p on next ch, 3 ds, 3 ps sep by 3 ds, 2 ds, cl, rw. * (Ch of 3 ds, 4 ps sep by 3 ds, 3 ds, rw. R of 2 ds, p, 3 ds, join to corresponding p on last r, 3 ds, 4 ps sep by 3 ds, 2 ds, cl, rw) 5 times. Ch as before. R of 2 ds, p, 3 ds, join to corresponding p on last r, 3 ds, p, 3 ds, join to last p of next ch on previous row, 3 ds, join to first p on next ch, 3 ds, p, 2 ds, cl, rw. Ch of 3 ds, 6 ps sep by 3 ds, 3 ds, * * rw. R of 2 ds, p, 3 ds, miss 5 ps on previous row, join to next p, 3 ds, join to first p on next ch, 3 ds, 3 ps sep by 3 ds, 2 ds, cl, rw; repeat from * ending last repeat at * * and joining last ch to base of first r. Tie ends, cut and oversew neatly on wrong side. Damp and pin out to measurements.

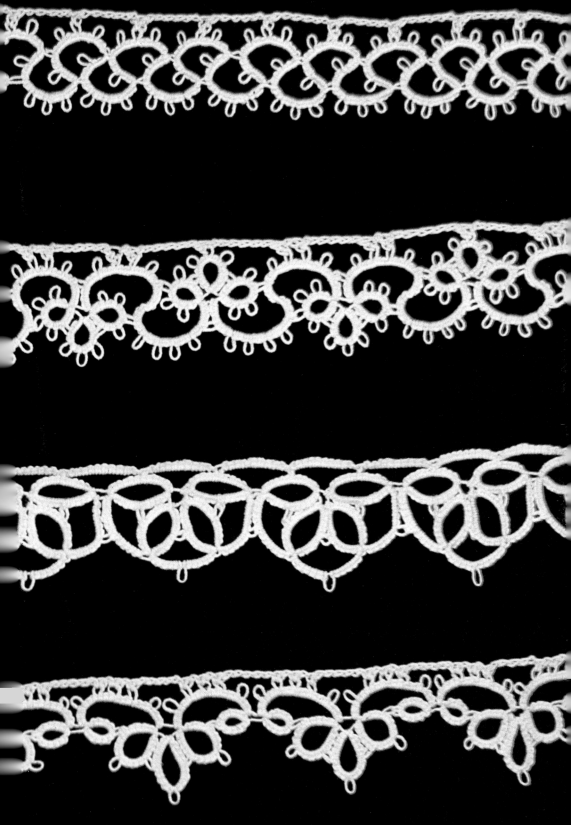

Four edgings

Materials: Coats Mercer-Crochet no. 10, 20, 40, or 60.
Milward tatting shuttle.
Milward steel crochet hook.

Edging 1

Tie ball and shuttle threads together. R of 3 ds, 5 ps sep by 2 ds, 3 ds, cl. (R of 3 ds, join to last p of previous r, 2 ds, 4 ps sep by 2 ds, 3 ds, cl) twice, rw. Ch of 4 ds, 6 ps sep by 3 ds, 4 ds, rw. * Ch of 4 ds, join to 3rd p of last r, 3 ds, 5 ps sep by 3 ds, 4 ds, rw. R of 3 ds, 2 ps sep by 2 ds, 2 ds, join to last p of adjacent ch, 2 ds, 2 ps sep by 2 ds, 3 ds, cl. (R of 3 ds, join to last p of previous r, 2 ds, 4 ps sep by 2 ds, 3 ds, cl) twice, rw. Ch of 4 ds, join to corresponding p of adjacent ch, 3 ds, 5 ps sep by 3 ds, 4 ds, row; repeat from * for length required, ending to correspond with beginning. Tie ends, cut and oversew neatly on wrong side.

Crochet heading

Attach thread to centre p of second r worked, 1 dc into same place as join, * (6 ch, 1 dc into second p of next ch, 1 ch, 1 dc into next p on same ch) twice, 6 ch, 1 dc into centre p of next r; repeat from * to end. Fasten off.

for colour illustration, see page 119

dging 2

e ball and shuttle threads together. Ch of
ds, 5 ps sep by 3 ds, 3 ds, rw. * Ch of 3 ds, 5 ps
p by 3 ds, 3 ds, miss 1 p on previous ch, join
shuttle thread to next p, rw; repeat from *
r length required. Tie ends, cut and oversew
atly on wrong side.

ochet heading

tach thread to centre p of last ch of edging,
lc into same place as join, * 6 ch, 1 dc into
ntre free p of next ch; repeat from * to end.
asten off.

dging 3

t row: Tie ball and shuttle threads to-
ther. R of 6 ds, p, 6 ds, lp, 6 ds, p, 6 ds, cl, rw.
h of 6 ds, p, 6 ds, rw. * R of 6 ds, join to last p
previous r, 6 ds, join to lp of previous r, 6 ds,
6 ds, cl, rw. Ch of 6 ds, p, 6 ds, rw. R of 6 ds,
in to last p of previous r, 6 ds, join to same lp
last r was joined, 6 ds, p, 6ds, cl, rw. Ch of
ds, p, 6 ds, rw. R of 6 ds, join to last p of pre-
ous r, 6 ds, join to same lp as previous r was
ined, 6 ds, p, 6 ds, cl. R of 6 ds, p, 6 ds, lp, 6 ds,
6 ds, cl, rw. Ch of 6 ds, join to p of adja-
nt ch, 6 ds, rw; repeat from * for length
quired, ending to correspond with begin-
ng. Tie ends, cut and oversew neatly on
rong side.

id row: Tie ball and shuttle threads to p of
st r of previous row, * 10 ds, join by shuttle
read to p of next r of previous row; repeat
om * to end. Tie ends, cut and oversew
atly on wrong side.

Edging 4

Tie ball and shuttle threads together. R of 5
ds, 3 ps sep by 5 ds, 5 ds, cl. * (R of 5 ds, join to
last p of previous r, 5 ds, 2 ps sep by 5 ds, 5 ds,
cl) twice, rw. Ch of 3 ds, 5 ps sep by 3 ds, 3 ds,
rw. R of 6 ds, join to last p of previous r, 6 ds,
cl. R of 6 ds, p, 6 ds, cl, rw. Ch of 3 ds, 5 ps sep
by 3 ds, 3 ds, rw. R of 5 ds, join to p of previous
r, 5 ds, 2 ps sep by 5 ds, 5 ds, cl; repeat from *
for length required, ending to correspond with
beginning. Tie ends, cut and oversew neatly
on wrong side.

Crochet heading

Attach thread to first p of first r, 8 ch, miss one
p of first ch, 1 ss into next p, * (1 ch, 1 ss into
next p) twice, 5 ch, miss next 2 ps, 1 ss into
next p; repeat from * ending last repeat with
5 ch, miss next p, 1 tr into next p, Fasten off.

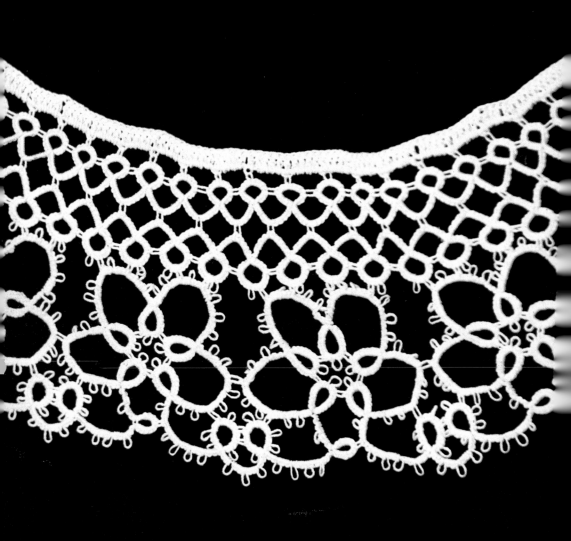

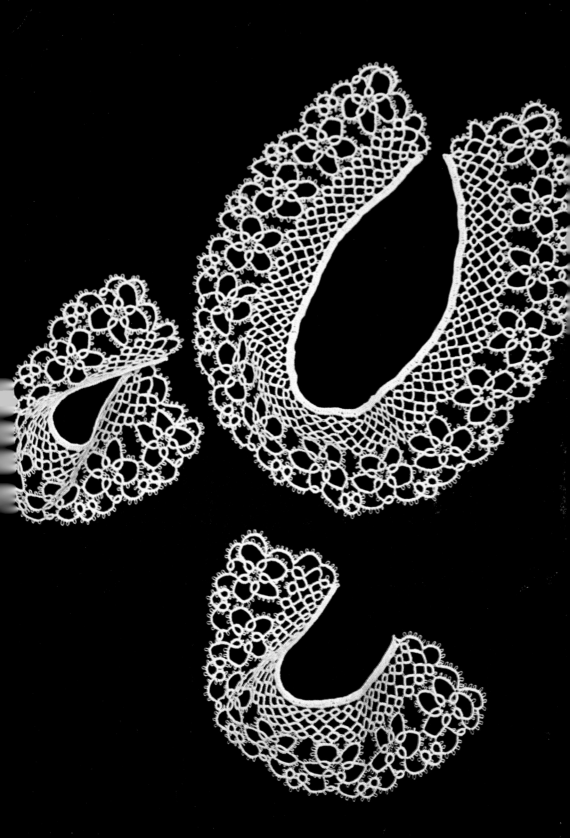

Collar and cuff set

Materials: Coats Mercer-Crochet no. 40
(20 grms).
1 ball. This model is worked in White.
Milward steel crochet hook 1·00 (no. 4).
Milward tatting shuttle.

Depth of edging: 2½ ins.

for detail, see page 122
for colour illustration, page 123

Collar

1st row: Tie ball and shuttle threads together. R of 4 ds, 3 ps sep by 4 ds, 4 ds, cl. * Rw,
ch of 5 ds, p, 5 ds, rw. R of 4 ds, join to last p of
previous r, 4 ds, 2 ps sep by 4 ds, 4 ds, cl; repeat
from * 56 times more. (58 rings.)

2nd row: Ch of 8 ds, p, 8 ds. R of 5 ds, p, 5 ds, p,
2 ds, p, 5 ds, p, 5 ds, cl. * Rw, ch of 5 ds, join to
p of ch on previous row, 5 ds, rw. R of 5 ds,
join to last p of previous r, 5 ds, p, 2 ds, p, 5 ds,
p, 5 ds, cl; repeat from * to end, ch of 8 ds, p,
8 ds, join to base of first r on previous row. Tie
ends, cut and oversew neatly on wrong side.

3rd row: Tie ball and shuttle threads together. Attach thread to centre p of last r on
first row. Ch of 3 ds, 5 ps sep by 3 ds, 3 ds, join
by shuttle thread to p of next ch on previous
row, 3 ds, 6 ps sep by 3 ds, 3 ds, join by shuttle
thread to 2nd free p of first r on previous row,
3 ds, 7 ps sep by 3 ds, 3 ds, leave small sp, 3 ds,
7 ps sep by 3 ds, 3 ds, leave small sp, 3 ds, 4 ps
sep by 3 ds, 3 ds. Sr of 6 ds, p, 6 ds, cl. Ch of 3
ds, p, 3 ds. R of 8 ds, 3 ps sep by 2 ds, 8 ds, cl,
rw. Ch of 3 ds, 3 ps sep by 3 ds, 3 ds, join to
small sp, 3 ds, 4 ps sep by 3 ds, 3 ds, join to
next small sp, rw. R of 8 ds, join to last p on
previous r, 2 ds, p, 2 ds, p, 8 ds, cl, rw. Ch of 3
ds, 4 ps sep by 3 ds, 3 ds, join to next free p on
last r on previous row, 3 ds, 3 ps sep by 3 ds,
3 ds, rw. R of 8 ds, join to last free p on previous r, 2 ds, p, 2 ds, p, 8 ds, cl, rw. Ch of 3 ds,
3 ps sep by 3 ds, 3 ds, miss 1 r on previous
row, join to first free p on next r, 3 ds, 4 ps sep
by 3 ds, 3 ds, rw. R of 8 ds, join to last p on previous r, 2 ds, p, 2 ds, p, 8 ds, cl, rw. Ch of 3 ds,
8 ps sep by 3 ds, 3 ds, rw. R of 8 ds, join to last p
on previous r, 2 ds, p, 2 ds, join to first p on
first r, 8 ds, cl. * Ch of 3 ds, p, 3 ds, join to p on
sr, 3 ds, 4 ps sep by 3 ds, 3 ds, rw. R of 2 ds, p,

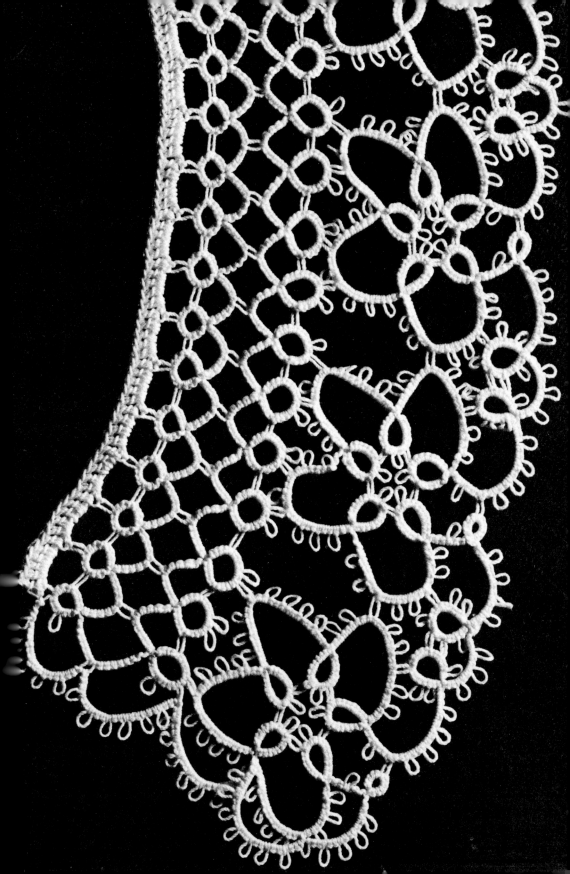

3 ds, p, 3 ds, miss 2 ps on last 8 p ch, join to next p, 3 ds, 4 ps sep by 3 ds, 2 ds, cl, rw. Ch of 3 ds, 3 ps sep by 3 ds, 3 ds, rw. R of 2 ds, p, 3 ds, join to 2nd p of last r, 3 ds, join to next p of last r, 3 ds, 4 ps sep by 3 ds, 2 ds, cl, rw. Ch of 3 ds, 4 ps sep by 3 ds, 3 ds. Sr of 6 ds, p, 6 ds, cl. Ch of 3 ds, p, 3 ds. * * R of 8 ds, 3 ps sep by 2 ds, 8 ds, cl, rw. Ch of 3 ds, 2 ps sep by 3 ds, 3 ds, join to 3rd p of adjacent r, 3 ds, 2 ps sep by 3 ds, 3 ds, join to corresponding p on adjacent ch, 3 ds, 2 ps sep by 3 ds, 3 ds, rw. R of 8 ds, join to last p of previous r, 2 ds, p, 2 ds, p, 8 ds, cl, rw. Ch of 3 ds, 3 ps sep by 3 ds, 3 ds, join to 2nd free p of next r on previous row, 3 ds, p, 3 ds, join to first free p of next r on previous row, 3 ds, 2 ps sep by 3 ds, 3 ds, rw. R of 8 ds, join to last p on previous r, 2 ds, p, 2 ds, p, 8 ds, cl, rw. Ch of 3 ds, 2 ps sep by 3 ds, 3 ds, miss 1 p on next r on previous row, join to next p, 3 ds, p, 3 ds, join to first free p on next r on previous row, 3 ds, 3 ps sep by 3 ds, 3 ds, rw. R of 8 ds, join to last p on previous r, 2 ds, p, 2 ds, p, 8 ds, cl, rw. Ch of 3 ds, 8 ps sep by 3 ds, 3 ds, rw. R of 8 ds, join to last p of previous r, 2 ds, p, 2 ds, join to first p of adjacent r, 8 ds, cl; repeat from * until 3 rs remain on previous row then repeat from * to * * once. R of 8 ds, 3 ps sep by 2 ds, 8 ds, cl, rw. Ch of 3 ds, 2 ps sep by 3 ds, 3 ds, join to 3rd p of adjacent r, 3 ds, 2 ps sep by 3 ds, 3 ds, miss 2 ps on adjacent ch, join to next p, 3 ds, 2 ps sep by 3 ds, 3 ds, rw. R of 8 ds, join to last p on previous r, 2 ds, p, 2 ds, p, 8 ds, cl, rw. Ch of 3 ds, 4 ps sep by 3 ds, 3 ds, miss 1 p on next r on previous row, join to next p, 3 ds, 3 ps sep by 3 ds, 3 ds, rw. R of 8 ds, join to last p on previous r, 2 ds, p, 2 ds, p, 8 ds, cl, rw. Ch of 3 ds, 3 ps sep by 3 ds, miss 1 r on previous row, join to p on next r, 3 ds, 4 ps sep by 3 ds, 3 ds, rw. R of 8 ds join to last p of previous r, 2 ds, 2 ps sep by 2 ds, 8 ds, cl, rw. Ch of 3 ds, 8 ps sep by 3 ds, 3 ds, rw. R of 8 ds, join to last p of previous r,

2 ds, p, 2 ds, join to first p of adjacent r, 8 ds, cl. Ch of 3 ds, p, 3 ds, join to p of sr, 3 ds, 4 ps sep by 3 ds, 3 ds, miss 3 ps on last 8 p ch, join by shuttle thread to next p, 3 ds, 7 ps sep by 3 ds, 3 ds, join by shuttle thread to base of second last r worked, 3 ds, 7 ps sep by 3 ds, 3 ds, join by shuttle thread to first free p of next r on 2nd row, 3 ds, 6 ps sep by 3 ds, 3 ds, join by shuttle thread to p on next ch on last row, 3 ds, 5 ps sep by 3 ds, 3 ds, join to centre p on first r on first row. Tie ends, cut and oversew neatly on wrong side.

Cuffs *make 2*

1st row: Tie ball and shuttle threads together. R of 4 ds, 3 ps sep by 4 ds, 4 ds, cl. * Rw, ch of 5 ds, p, 5 ds, rw. R of 4 ds, join to last p of previous r, 4 ds, 2 ps sep by 4 ds, 4 ds, cl; repeat from * 24 times more. (26 rings.)

2nd row: Ch of 8 ds, p, 8 ds. R of 5 ds, p, 5 ds, p, 2 ds, p, 5 ds, p, 5 ds, cl. * Rw, ch of 5 ds, join to p of ch on previous row, 5 ds, rw. R of 5 ds, join to last p of previous r, 5 ds, p, 2 ds, p, 5 ds, p, 5 ds, cl; repeat from * to end, ch of 8 ds, p, 8 ds, join to base of first r on previous row. Tie ends, cut and oversew neatly on wrong side.

3rd row: As 3rd row of collar.

Crochet heading for collars and cuffs.
1st row: Join thread to same p as last ch on last row, 1 dc into p, * 4 ch, 1 dc into next p; repeat from * ending with 3 ch, turn.

2nd row: * 4 tr into next sp, 1 tr into next dc; repeat from * to end of row. Fasten off. Damp and pin out to measurements.

Cheval set in two colours

Materials: Coats Mercer-Crochet no. 20 (20 grms).
2 balls each Buttercup and Dk Ecru.
Milward tatting shuttle.

Size of motif: 2 ins square.

Measurements: Centrepiece – 10 × 18 ins.
Small mat – 8 × 12 ins.

Centrepiece

First motif

Wind approximately ¾ yd of Dk Ecru on to shuttle. Work a centre r of 2 ds, 8 ps sep by 3 ds, 1 ds, cl. Tie ends, cut and oversew neatly on wrong side.

Wind shuttle with Buttercup and, using Dk Ecru ball, tie ball and shuttle threads together. R of 4 ds, 2 ps sep by 4 ds, 2 ds, join to any p of centre r, 2 ds, 2 ps sep by 4 ds, 4 ds, cl, rw. * Ch of 5 ds, 3 ps sep by 5 ds, 5 ds, rw. R of 4 ds, p, 4 ds, join to 2nd last p of previous r, 2 ds, join to next p on centre r, 2 ds, 2 ps sep by 4 ds, 4 ds, cl, rw. Ch of 5 ds, rw. Sr of 4 ds, p, 4 ds, cl, rw. Ch of 10 ds, p, 10 ds, rw. Sr of 4 ds, join to p of previous sr, 4 ds, cl, rw. Ch of 5 ds, rw. R of 4 ds, p, 4 ds, join to 2nd last p of previous r, 2 ds, join to next p on centre r, 2 ds, 2 ps sep by 4 ds, 4 ds, cl, rw; repeat from * 3 times more, omitting r at end of last repeat, joining last r worked to first r and last ch to base of first r. Tie ends, cut and oversew neatly on wrong side.

Second motif

Work as for first motif to end of first sr, rw. Ch of 10 ds, join to p of any corresponding ch on first motif, 10 ds, rw. Work as before to end of next r, rw. Ch of 5 ds, p, 5 ds, join to centre of next corresponding ch on first motif, 5 ds, p, 5 ds, rw. Work as before to end of next sr, rw. Ch of 10 ds, join to p of next corresponding ch on first motif, 10 ds, rw. Complete motif as before. Tie ends, cut and oversew neatly on wrong side.
Work 5 rows of 9 motifs, joining adjacent sides as second motif was joined to first motif.

Small mat *make 2*

Work 4 rows of 6 motifs, joining as before. Damp and press.

for colour illustration, see page 127